HELPING HANDS

HOME TO HEATHER CREEK

HELPING HANDS

Carolyne Aarsen

Home to Heather Creek is a trademark of Guideposts.

Copyright © 2024 by Guideposts. All rights reserved.

This book, or parts thereof, may not be reproduced, stored in a retrieval system, or transmitted in any form or by any means, electronic, mechanical, photocopying, recording, or otherwise, without the written permission of the publisher.

The characters and events in this book are fictional, and any resemblance to actual persons or occurrences is coincidental.

Scripture quotations in this volume are taken from the *The Holy Bible, New International Version* (NIV). Copyright © 1973, 1978, 1984, 2011 by Biblica, Inc. Used by permission of Zondervan. All rights reserved worldwide.

Published by Guideposts
100 Reserve Road, Suite E200
Danbury, CT 06810
Guideposts.org

Cover by Lookout Design, Inc.
Interior design by Cindy LaBreacht
Additional design work by Müllerhaus
Typeset by Aptara, Inc.

ISBN 978-1-961125-23-0 (hardcover)
ISBN 978-1-961125-25-4 (epub)

Printed in the United States of America
10 9 8 7 6 5 4 3 2 1

Acknowledgments

I'd like to dedicate this book to Linda Ford, my writing partner, brainstormer extraordinaire and dear friend. I couldn't do this writing thing without you.

As well I want to thank Beth Adams, Fiona Serpa and all the people at Guideposts Books for guiding us authors through this series with wisdom, tact and skill and making this series a joy to read. Blessings on you all.

—Carolyne Aarsen

Home to Heather Creek

Before the Dawn

Sweet September

Circle of Grace

Homespun Harvest

A Patchwork Christmas

An Abundance of Blessings

Every Sunrise

The Promise of Spring

April's Hope

Seeds of Faith

On the Right Path

Sunflower Serenade

Second Chances

Prayers and Promises

Giving Thanks

Holiday Homecoming

Family Matters

All Things Hidden

To Love and Cherish

A Time to Grow

Sentimental Journey

Helping Hands

HELPING HANDS

Chapter One

Not again.

Charlotte held up Christopher's newest pants and sighed. Another hole in another knee after he'd already ripped two pairs of pants this week.

She tossed them in the washing machine and turned it on. She'd have to have a chat with him about being more careful. He had older clothes to wear for his chores.

As the machine filled with water, she took the other clothes out of the dryer. As she folded, her mind ticked over the jobs for the day. She'd have to get Emily and Christopher to help her in the garden. It needed weeding again. And the windows outside needed washing. She had promised her sister-in-law, Rosemary, that she would help her set up a quilting display in her fabric store later this afternoon. Also, her dear friend Hannah had been under the weather the past few days, and Charlotte had said she would visit.

Her son Bill, his wife Anna, and their two girls and baby boy were coming for dinner on Sunday after church, and there was cleaning and baking to be done.

On top of that, somehow she had to find a way to keep her grandchildren busy for the rest of the summer. Though it was their second year of living on the farm, they still needed a prod now and again to get things done.

She rolled up a pair of socks and set them on Sam's pile of clothes in the laundry basket, picked it up, and walked into the kitchen.

She frowned at what she saw.

A bowl sat on the counter, the mixer lying at a haphazard angle beside it. The milk and eggs stood to one side, and bananas, already peeled, lay on the countertop. Where was Emily? The banana bread Charlotte had asked her to make was supposed to be baking in the oven by now along with a batch of cookies.

Charlotte glanced over to the family room, but the only person there was Sam, hunched over the screen of the computer.

"Sam, what game are you playing?"

"I'm not playing," he muttered. "Grandpa sent me in here to look for some silly part for the haybine. He said to look on this one site, but I can't figure out what he wants."

"What's wrong with it?" Charlotte felt dread at Sam's words. All week Bob and their son Pete had been fretting about cutting the hay and a host of other things that needed to be done immediately. As a true farmer's wife, Charlotte often took on the same worries as her husband and son. The farm's livelihood was everyone's concern. "Do you think you'll be able to find it?"

The only reply she received was Sam's laconic shrug.

"Do you need me to run into town for anything?"

Sam leaned closer to the screen and shook his head. "I don't even know what we need yet. I've gotta teach

Grandpa how to work this thing so I don't have to do this," he muttered again.

"I thought Christopher gave him a few lessons awhile ago," Charlotte recalled.

"Yeah, well, they didn't seem to sink in," Sam replied.

"Where is Christopher anyway?" Charlotte wondered out loud.

"Haven't seen the little dude all morning," Sam said.

"I thought he went outside with you after breakfast."

"He did, but Uncle Pete wouldn't let him drive the tractor, so he took off."

"You said you would watch him," Charlotte said, trying not to express her annoyance. She glanced back at the milk still sitting out and went back to put it in the fridge. In this heat it would go sour in no time.

"I did. And then he took off so I couldn't watch him anymore." Sam leaned closer to the screen, sighed, and shook his head as he navigated to another page.

"And you don't know where he went?" Charlotte pressed, picking up the eggs as well.

"I told you, Grandma. I haven't seen him since Uncle Pete said he couldn't drive the tractor."

Charlotte stopped herself from reprimanding her grandson. Sam had been testy the past few days, and Charlotte knew he struggled with his own set of worries.

College lay ahead of him. His girlfriend, Arielle, was heading off to Grace University in Omaha while he would be staying home and commuting to Central Community College in Grand Island.

Charlotte knew Sam wondered how he and Arielle

would manage the separation and how they would maintain the relationship over the distance.

Charlotte had her own concerns about Sam. It had taken him some time to decide where he would go to school and what he would take. The brief return of their estranged father into the children's lives at Christmastime hadn't helped Sam's equilibrium.

She just hoped and prayed he wouldn't change his mind about college, even though there was some concern about how it would get paid for.

Now the haybine was broken down...

Stop! Charlotte told herself. How many times had she worried about the farm? About the children? About how she and Bob would cope with taking care of grandchildren who barely knew them when they first came to the farm? How many times had she worried about their lives, the big and little things?

In spite of her years, it seemed she still had to trust God daily that they would be given strength to handle whatever came their way.

Sam muttered some more, but Charlotte chose to ignore it. She had to deal with Emily now.

"Emily, where are you?" she called, setting the bananas on a plate.

"Sorry, Grandma," Emily answered, running down the stairs, phone in hand. "I was...uh...talking on the phone."

Charlotte gave her an *are-you-kidding-me?* look, one she had learned from Emily. "Who or what was more important than baking banana bread?" she asked as she washed her hands.

"Well, you see...," Emily started.

Charlotte had a pretty good idea of what had happened. Troy again.

When Emily and Troy first started dating, Charlotte and Bob had had their doubts. Troy wasn't exactly boyfriend material, yet he was kind to Emily and seemed to be improving in nature.

And he loved talking to Emily on the phone.

"Surely you can talk to your boyfriend and mix dough at the same time?"

"She could, but she didn't want me listening in," Sam said.

Emily just rolled her eyes in another classic teenager move.

Then the porch door slammed, and Christopher burst into the kitchen. "I thought the banana bread would be ready by now," he said.

Charlotte had to smile at how quickly her other small worry had been eased away. Christopher was obviously fine.

"It's coming, it's coming," Emily grumbled, dumping the bananas into the bowl.

"I was hoping for some banana bread too," Sam said, scribbling something down on a piece of paper beside the computer.

"Oh, you never mind. If you and Arielle ever get married, you might have to learn to bake banana bread yourself," Emily retorted.

"Great big emphasis on the *if*." Sam stood up, shoved the chair under the computer desk, slapped his hat on his head, and slouched out the door.

"I wish Sam wasn't so grumpy," Christopher said, walking over to the cookie jar and lifting the lid. "This is empty too?"

Charlotte ignored his complaint. "Sam is worried about college. And if you don't have anything to do, Christopher, I'd like you to help me in the garden."

Christopher made a face. "Why can't Emily help you?"

"Emily *is* helping me," Charlotte said, "as soon as she's done baking the banana bread and cookies I asked her to make."

Charlotte caught the tail end of Emily's eye roll and chose to ignore it. There was a time when that would have really annoyed her, but taking care of teenage grandchildren had taught her the valuable lesson of choosing which battles to fight and which ones to let slide.

The phone rang and Emily dove for it. Then she made a face, covered the phone, and handed it to Charlotte. "It's for you, Grandma."

Charlotte took the phone but first glanced at her grandson. "You get started, Christopher, and I'll be there as soon as I'm done with this phone call."

"Hello?" she said, answering the call and simultaneously organizing the loose papers that had gravitated to the desk near the cordless phone's base. Every day more mail was added to the pile, and the job of sorting through it all always fell to her.

"Charlotte? Oh, Charlotte, I need to talk to you. I need you."

"Hannah? Did something happen? Are you okay?" The frantic voice on the other end was almost unrecognizable as that of her dear friend and neighbor. "Hannah, calm down. What's wrong?"

"I'm at the hospital in Harding. You have to come."

Charlotte's heart leapt into her throat. "What happened? What's going on?"

"It's Frank. He's had a heart attack."

"YOU SURE I CAN'T HAVE another cookie?" Christopher stared longingly at the pile of cookies Emily carefully placed in the cookie jar.

"You've already had four," Emily said, flicking her fingers at his hands as he tried to sneak another one. "I don't want you to spoil your appetite."

"Do you think Grandma will be back in time to make supper?" Christopher licked the chocolate off his fingers and pressed his thumb down on some errant crumbs on the countertop.

"I'm not sure." As soon as Grandma got to the hospital, she had phoned Emily to tell her she would be there a while. That was three hours ago, and it was getting close to suppertime.

"If Grandma doesn't come home on time, what are you making for supper?" Christopher asked, sweeping the rest of the crumbs into his cupped hand and tossing them into his mouth. "Can we have cereal? And can we watch TV when we eat?"

Emily bit her lip as she glanced at the clock. She had finished baking the cookies and had taken the clothes out of the dryer and folded them. She and Christopher had weeded the garden and kept busy while waiting for Grandma to come back.

But she still wasn't home, and suppertime was creeping closer.

"No, we can't have cereal. Grandpa and Sam will be hungry after working all day outside." Emily tapped her finger against her lip, trying to think.

The phone rang, and she jumped to answer it, hoping it would be Grandma saying she was coming home.

But it was Ashley.

"Hey, friend," Emily said. "What are you up to?"

"Remember that Bible camp thing I told you about that we were too late to sign up for? Camp Whispering Pines? I heard there were some last-minute openings so I got a couple of application forms. You wanna come?"

Emily frowned. When Ashley brought it up toward the end of the school year, Emily hadn't been too stoked about the idea, mostly because she was ashamed to admit she had no idea what Bible camp was. So she had been kind of glad there weren't any openings then.

"I don't know."

"I mean, you don't need to come..."

Emily sensed Ashley's disappointment and wished she could be more excited. "Well, it's just I've never been to a Bible camp. What do you do all day? Read the Bible?"

Ashley laughed. "Of course not. There are a lot of other things to do. Hiking, canoeing, horseback riding, swimming. We play games, do crafts—hey, I know it sounds lame, but it's really a lot of fun."

"No, if that's what it's like, it sounds like it could be

great." Anytime she could get away from the farm and her brothers was a good time. "You should have told me the first time."

"Sorry. I . . . uh . . . I just thought you would know."

"I grew up in San Diego, remember? Mom was too broke to send us anywhere."

Though it had been a couple of years since her mother died, Emily still felt a gentle pang whenever she thought of her. It didn't hurt as much as it had the first half year after she and her brothers had moved to the farm to live with their grandparents. But it still hurt.

"Sorry. I keep forgetting. Sometimes I think you've been here all your life."

"Where does the Bible part come in?" Emily tucked the cordless phone between her ear and her shoulder as she dug through the freezer, hoping that by some miracle Grandma had a casserole hidden away among the packages of meat and bread and assorted frozen goods.

No such luck.

"Well, there's usually a speaker in the evening who talks about different parts of our faith life," Ashley said. "And we sing songs around the campfire and do devotions every morning."

Emily closed the freezer and walked back into the kitchen, listening and thinking at the same time. Christopher was in the family room playing on the computer. He wasn't supposed to be on the computer in the middle of the day, but summer days on the farm kind of stretched out and could get boring.

She wasn't going to tell him he couldn't, not after he

had helped her weed the garden in the hot June sun. Suddenly the thought of being on a lake sounded pretty cool, in every meaning of the word.

"I'm not much for that kind of stuff, but I'd put up with it so I could do all the other things." When Emily, Sam, and Christopher lived in San Diego they had never gone to church, but since moving here, they'd gone every Sunday with Grandma and Grandpa. Rules of the house.

Emily understood church and God were important. Once in a while, when she was really scared or confused—like when their dad, who hadn't seen them in years, came to visit last Christmas—she felt like praying. And the few times she did pray after that, it seemed like maybe someone was listening.

So maybe the Bible part could be okay.

"If you want to go, that'd be awesome," Ashley was saying. "I don't feel like going if you're not."

"I think I'd like to go." Then Emily had another thought. "But what about Troy? He never said anything about coming. Would he want to?"

"You don't have to do everything with your boyfriend," Ashley said with a sigh. Ashley and her boyfriend Ryan had broken up awhile back, and Emily knew she was feeling a bit out of sorts that Emily and Troy were going pretty strong.

"How long is this camp anyway?" Emily asked.

"Ten days."

"That's a long time to be gone," Emily said. "I wonder if that's such a good idea."

"You'd rather be at home, milking the cow, gathering

eggs, and weeding the garden while I'm out riding horses, paddling a canoe, and working on my tan?"

Emily leaned on the counter and looked out the window overlooking the garden, which would need weeding again in a week or so. She thought of the chores she had to do every day and how boring it could get on the farm.

"And besides," Ashley continued, "Troy will miss you and when you come home he'll be all smoochy and clingy and huggy. How can that be bad?"

Emily had to laugh at the thought. Troy was a great guy, but he wasn't one for much affection.

"Might be good for him if you're gone for a bit," Ashley said. "Maybe he'll realize how lucky he is to have you."

"Or maybe I'll realize how lucky I am to have him," Emily said, a flash of reality hitting her. "What does this camp cost?"

"Nothing. The church pays for kids from our congregation to attend."

"Really? It's free?" Well, that settled it. "I'm so coming," Emily said.

"You will?" Ashley squealed in Emily's ear. "That's great. Awesome. Amazing. You won't regret this. It will be so much fun. Now we need to make plans. I can drop the forms off today, and the lady who takes them said that was okay. Your grandma will probably have to sign something, but I'm sure they'll reserve your space."

"When do we have to be there?"

"The bus leaves Monday afternoon. Camp starts Monday night."

"How far away is it?"

"Only an hour."

"Awesome." Emily was getting more excited about the idea all the time.

Then Emily glanced at the clock, and her heart jumped. "Rats. Ashley, I gotta go. I have to make supper, and I have no idea what to make."

"Where's your Grandma?"

"She had to go to the hospital with our neighbor Hannah, and she's not back yet. And Grandpa and Sam and Uncle Pete have been working outside all day so I know they'll be hungry." The more she talked, the more panicky she got. "And if they're hungry and I don't have anything to make them—"

"Why don't you make sloppy joes? Or chili?" Ashley suggested.

"Nah, it's too hot for that. Maybe I could make pasta with some vegetables."

"Sounds good to me," Ashley offered.

"Okay, well, if I gotta cook this stuff, I better get going."

"Don't forget to ask your grandma about the camp thing."

"I won't. I'm pretty pumped." Emily felt a shiver of excitement at the idea of being away from the farm for ten days. It would be so much fun.

"We can get together tomorrow and make plans," Ashley said. "Get Sam to drive you if you can't borrow your grandma's car."

"Excellent idea," Emily said. She said good-bye to her friend and grinned. Ten days away from Sam, Christopher, and the farm.

It was going to be so, so cool.

Twenty minutes later, she had pasta boiling on the stove and was mixing some garlic butter to spread on the bread she would heat up. The whole time she worked, she imagined being at camp, meeting new people, and having a new adventure.

Then, while she checked the pasta, misgivings nudged at her. Would Grandma really let her be away for ten days? Even if she was going to Bible camp?

What could she do to convince Grandma to let her go?

She put the wooden spoon down on the spoon rest and suddenly had a brainstorm. If she cleaned the house and folded the laundry, Grandma would be so impressed with her. And if she was impressed, she'd be in a good mood when Emily asked her about camp. Then she'd probably let her go.

Genius. Sheer genius, Emily thought, starting with the kitchen counters.

Chapter Two

"I could have stayed at my place," Hannah said as Charlotte turned into the driveway of the farm. "I don't need to stay with you."

"I'm not taking you back to your house to stay. You're not feeling well, and I don't want you to be alone," Charlotte insisted as she parked the car by the house. She had taken Hannah by her own house to pick up a few things but insisted she get back in the car with her and come to Heather Creek Farm for the night.

Charlotte's voice was firm, but deep inside, she stifled a beat of despair. She'd dropped everything to rush to the hospital to help her friend, leaving chaos behind. Sitting around Harding Memorial, waiting for doctors' reports, had drained what little energy she had left.

When Charlotte got to the hospital, she had found Hannah pacing the hall outside the ICU, her face pale, a sheen of sweat on her brow. When Hannah spotted Charlotte, she'd run toward her and clung to her like a sailor grasping a mast in a wild storm.

Charlotte had stayed by her friend's side as they waited for the heart specialist to show up, but all they learned was what they already suspected: Frank had suffered a heart attack, but he was stable for now. They would have to do further tests to determine if he would need surgery. The nurses had informed Hannah that she couldn't stay over at the hospital, so it only made sense to go home and get some rest for the days ahead. She had protested, but the nurses assured her they would contact her if Frank's condition changed.

Now Hannah dragged her hands through her graying hair. "Are you sure it's okay to stay with you and Bob? I don't want to put anybody out."

"You won't be putting anyone out. No one is in the spare room anymore," Charlotte said, giving her dear friend a gentle smile.

"I should have changed when I was at home," Hannah said, pulling at her sweatshirt.

The words LIVE FOR TODAY marched across her blue sweatshirt in poufy pink letters, a touch of irony, given the situation. The sweatshirt still carried a dusting of flour and berry stains from the pie Hannah had been making when Frank collapsed on the kitchen floor in front of her. Charlotte had helped her clean up the abandoned pie when they went back to get Hannah's clothes and toiletries.

"You can change after a hot bath. Just come into the house." Charlotte hadn't had time to call home again after her first quick call when she'd arrived at the hospital. Now she realized too late that she should have picked up something for supper from Mel's Diner as they drove home.

The thought of the work still awaiting her almost made her stumble in her weariness—a weariness she didn't dare show in front of her friend for fear of making her feel guilty. But when Charlotte opened the porch door and caught the aroma of supper cooking, she felt a pulse of gratitude.

She stepped into the kitchen, pleased to see her family sitting around the table, already eating. They all looked up as Charlotte and Hannah arrived, and Bob stood up from his chair.

"How is Frank?" Bob gave Hannah an awkward hug and then stepped back.

Hannah pressed a hand against her face, shaking her head, unable to speak.

"He's stable for the time being. The doctors are consulting right now about what they will do next. We'll know more tomorrow," Charlotte said, slipping a comforting arm around her friend's shoulder. "Sam, why don't you get an extra chair from the family room?"

Sam did as he was asked, and Emily got up from the table too. "I'll get a couple of plates and some utensils. You sit down, Mrs. Carter. Sorry we didn't wait for you, Grandma, but we didn't know how long you would be."

"Do you need any help?" Charlotte asked.

"I've got everything under control," Emily said, giving her grandmother a quick smile. "You just sit down and take it easy."

"That would be lovely." Charlotte could feel the muscles in her neck relaxing as she dropped into her chair. A headache nagged at her temples, and she hoped, even prayed, that she wasn't getting whatever Hannah was fighting off. At least she didn't have to do anything. Emily was in charge.

As she watched her granddaughter in the kitchen, she realized how truly blessed she was.

"Hannah is staying for the night," Charlotte explained to the family, looking around the table.

"What is a heart attack?" Christopher asked as Emily set the plates in front of them.

Charlotte saw Sam elbow his little brother and then frown at him.

"Don't do that," Christopher complained. "I was just asking a question."

"Maybe Mrs. Carter doesn't want to talk about it," Sam hissed back.

"A heart attack can happen when one of the blood vessels to the heart is plugged by a clot and the heart muscle is damaged." Charlotte knew Christopher wouldn't quit asking questions until he got answers, and as painful as it was to talk about this in front of Hannah, it would be harder to keep Christopher at bay. "We can go look it up on the Internet after supper if you want," Charlotte said, glancing over at the computer.

"Did you get the haybine fixed, Bob?" Charlotte asked, steering the conversation in another direction.

"We phoned the company; they're sending in some parts. Sam can pick them up at AA tomorrow," Bob said. "By the way, the neighbors have all offered to pitch in and help with any work Frank needs done on the farm until he's able to get back to work."

"That's wonderful news, Bob," Charlotte said as Hannah forced a smile of gratitude.

They talked for a while, and then Emily spoke up. "Ashley called. She invited me to come to Bible camp."

Charlotte was momentarily taken aback. She didn't think Emily would enjoy that kind of thing. "When is that?"

"She's going to the first session? So it's going to start the beginning of next week? Monday or so?" Emily's voice lifted at the end of each comment, a sure sign that she really wanted to go.

"We'll talk about it later," Charlotte said, unable to make a decision on anything right now. She was thankful Emily got the hint and said nothing more.

Charlotte hoped that in a couple of days, Hannah would feel better. And she also hoped that Frank would be home as soon as possible.

For now, Charlotte knew she would need Emily's help. She wasn't so sure she should let Emily go.

Later. They would talk about camp later.

"How long do you have to work at the airport tomorrow?" Bob asked Sam, helping himself to another spoonful of pasta.

"I don't. I have to go check my hours though." Sam heaved a sigh. "It's hardly worth driving my car all the way out there just to work for a few bucks, but I really like working for Ed. I should ask for more hours." Sam folded his arms across his chest and tilted his chair back on two legs.

"You'll need money for college," Bob put in.

"Tell me about it." Sam sighed again. "Maybe I should just quit and find another job."

"Where would you work?" Charlotte asked. "It took you awhile to get *this* job."

Never mind that he had been irresponsible in his other job and as a consequence had lost it. His résumé was as spotty as a leopard.

Sam shrugged. "I don't know. I suppose I should check out the work situation in Harding."

"You'd have to earn good money to make the drive worth your while," Bob said.

"And if you don't put that chair down on four legs, you'll have to pay for it when it breaks," Emily added with a smirk.

"And if you don't stop being so bossy, I might have to go a round with you after supper."

"You wish."

Sam put the chair down, and the conversation shifted from his work to his plans for college, with Emily, Sam, and Christopher exchanging good-natured banter.

As the conversation shifted and changed, Charlotte glanced at her friend, thankful to see Hannah didn't look as pale and drawn as she had at the hospital. Her staying here was a good idea, Charlotte realized. The busyness of the Stevenson family was just what Hannah needed to keep her mind off Frank.

Supper was over, and Bob reached for the Bible. A silence settled over the room as he opened it. Bob licked his finger and turned a few pages, the rustling sound the only noise in the quiet. He cleared his throat, adjusted his glasses, and started reading, his voice deep and sure: "This is from Isaiah 49. I'm starting at verse 14." He waited a moment and then surreptitiously dabbed one corner of his eye.

Charlotte's heart swelled with love and compassion for her husband. Frank was Bob's dear friend, and the heart attack probably hit him very close to home. Bob's own health wasn't always the best, and with his diabetes, he was at a greater risk of having a heart attack as well. That his younger friend had suffered one was probably as much of a shock to him as it had been to Hannah.

Bob started reading, his voice sure.

"But Zion said, 'The LORD has forsaken me, the Lord has forgotten me.'

"'Can a mother forget the baby at her breast and have no compassion on the child she has borne? Though she may forget, I will not forget you! See, I have engraved you on the palms of my hands; your walls are ever before me.'"

Bob paused. "I'll stop there," he said, carefully closing the Bible. He took off his glasses, pinching the bridge of his nose, and then glanced around the table. "We can be thankful Frank is still with us and that God is holding him in the palms of his hands. We should continue to pray for him."

He waited a moment, cleared his throat again, and then lowered his head and prayed for a blessing on the work of the day, thanking God for the food and asking for strength and healing for Frank.

His prayer was simple, yet Charlotte knew it was heartfelt. When she raised her head, her eyes met his. She gave him a smile that encompassed all their own struggles, sorrows, and griefs, recognizing how God had helped through them all.

Bob's answering smile settled into her heart, reminding

her of what they had shared and continued to share, both with each other and with the grandchildren now sitting around their table.

The ringing of the phone pierced the moment, and Emily jumped to answer it.

"Don't tell me that Troy dearest is calling again," Sam said with a disgusted tone as he leaned back in his chair. "Doesn't that guy have anything else to do but call?"

"Did he call when I was out?" Charlotte asked.

"Every time I came into the house, Emily was chatting with him," Sam said, shaking his head. "I can't believe she doesn't have a sore ear."

"She got a lot of work done," Charlotte said, puzzled.

"She's really good at holding the phone between her shoulder and her ear," Christopher said. "That way she can get more done. And sometimes she puts it on speakerphone. Like when she folded laundry."

In spite of all the work Emily had done, Charlotte felt a niggling of concern at what she'd heard. She'd have to have a talk with Emily about Troy and set limits on phone time.

Emily returned, smiling, and put the phone back in the cradle.

"Wow, that was quick," Sam said. "Did you and Troy-boy run out of things to talk about?"

"That wasn't Troy," Emily said. "It was Ashley."

"Even more impressive," Sam said.

"I told her I had work to do and that I'd talk to her after I was done." Emily turned to Charlotte. "I'll take care of the dishes, Grandma. You and Mrs. Carter go sit in the family room."

"I think I'm going to bed instead, if you don't mind," Hannah said.

"I'll take you up." Charlotte got up, feeling every muscle in her body. She shot a thankful glance at Emily, who was already waving her hands at her in a shooing motion.

"When you come back down I'll make you some tea," Emily said.

"That sounds lovely." Charlotte gave her granddaughter a quick smile, once again thankful for the uncomplaining help she received.

Emily had come a long way since she first arrived as a resentful young girl. She was turning into a very responsible young woman.

Upstairs, Charlotte opened the door to the spare room and gave it a cursory glance. The blue quilt on the bed was smooth and neat; the room smelled fresh.

She brought Hannah's overnight bag into the room as Hannah dropped onto the bed.

"What a day," she said, letting her hands fall onto her lap. "I've never been so tired in all my life."

"You've been on an emotional roller coaster," Charlotte said, coming to sit beside her. She smoothed her friend's hair back from her face and picked up her worn hands to hold in hers. "That has to be exhausting, especially when you're not feeling well on top of everything else."

Hannah blinked, a single tear coursing down her slightly wrinkled cheek. "I just hate feeling this weepy. I know Frank and I aren't young anymore." She turned to Charlotte as another tear joined the first one glistening in the overhead light. "But it's hard to see him so helpless. I hate the thought that I had to leave him alone. I wish the hospital would allow spouses to stay overnight." She gave a short laugh. "We've rarely slept apart in all the years we've been married."

The anguish in her voice clutched at Charlotte's heart as she thought of how she would feel if it were Bob lying in the hospital instead of Frank. It was as if an icy finger feathered its way down her spine; she squeezed Hannah's hands even harder.

"We can be thankful he's in good hands and for now, he's okay," Charlotte assured her. "You and Frank love each other and, Lord willing, you'll have a lot of time left together." Charlotte paused. "Now I'd like to pray with you before you lie down."

Hannah nodded, and as Charlotte continued to hold Hannah's hands tightly between hers, the two friends bowed their heads.

"Dear Lord, thank You for sparing Frank's life today. We know our lives are in Your hands every day and that we take life for granted. We know how fragile our lives are, but yet Lord, we plead with You to be with Frank. Be with the doctors and nurses. May they help his recovery. We pray that he will be returned to Hannah and to us in Your time."

Charlotte paused, her own emotions threatening to overcome her, but she swallowed and continued. "Please give Hannah strength to get through this trial and help her to always trust in You and put her life in Your hands. Amen."

Charlotte waited a moment, praying silently for herself

—praying she could be a support to Hannah and thanking Him again that Emily could help her through this time.

"Do you need anything else?" Charlotte asked, squeezing her friend's hands one last time.

"No, I'm just going to take some pain reliever for this lousy headache."

"I'll put out some towels for you in the bathroom. If you need anything, just let Emily or me know."

Hannah nodded.

"Have a good sleep," Charlotte said, getting up and gently closing the door behind her.

Poor Hannah, she thought. *It's as if the ground has been cut out from under her.* She would really need Charlotte's support during the next chapter of her life.

Charlotte stopped at the bathroom, surprised to see the tidy counter and the shining sink. Emily had picked up the slack. The girl had even put out some towels and left a new bar of soap resting on top of them.

By the time she got downstairs the dishwasher was swishing through its cycle, and Emily was ordering her brothers around. Charlotte's burdens lifted off her shoulders.

In the family room she eased herself into her chair beside Bob's. She let out her breath in a gentle sigh and then glanced over at her husband.

"How are you?" she asked quietly.

Bob sat in his recliner holding the remote but staring sightlessly at the television's blank screen.

"This is a huge shock for us," she continued. "I never thought Frank would be the one—"

"It should have been me," Bob said, clenching his hand around the remote.

"Why do you say that?"

"I'm the one with the health problems." Bob raised and lowered his hand. "I'm the one who's at greater risk, and I'm nearly ten years older."

Charlotte did not know how to answer that. Instead, she wisely kept silent.

"It doesn't make any sense," Bob said. "Frank was always so healthy."

"He's still alive, Bob," Charlotte said, reaching over and resting her hand on his arm.

Bob shot her a frown; then, as what she was saying registered, he gave a short laugh. "Yes, yes. I know." He slowly shook his head back and forth. "But it just feels as if the shadow of death passed over our lives again. It was so hard losing Denise. I don't want to go through that sorrow again."

Charlotte gently stroked his arm, taking in the grease stains on his shirt, the frayed edges of his collar. Bob was a simple man. A farmer. He had a difficult time expressing his emotions. When they lost their daughter—Emily, Sam, and Christopher's mother—she and Bob had experienced deep, heartrending grief. While Charlotte had her friends to talk to about her pain, she knew Bob had kept his sorrow bottled deep within him.

"God brought us through that sorrow," she said quietly, still stroking his arm. "He'll bring us through whatever may lie ahead."

Bob nodded, releasing a deep sigh. "I know that's true. But we're both getting older, and so are our friends."

"For now we have each other." Charlotte got up and brushed a kiss over his grizzled cheeks. "And we have the children."

A gentle smile slipped over Bob's lips. "I'm so thankful God brought them into our lives."

As she picked up her knitting, Charlotte smiled. In spite of the frustrations, the children had kept them young, and they were an immense blessing in Charlotte's and Bob's lives.

And, Lord willing, they would continue to be.

Bob lifted the remote and clicked on the television, flicking through the channels, aimlessly searching for some entertainment.

When the children were done cleaning up, Sam and Christopher ambled outside, and Emily came into the family room.

"Thank you so much for helping out so well," Charlotte said, smiling at her granddaughter as she dropped onto the worn couch.

"Gladly done." Emily leaned back against the cushions, her hands folded over her stomach. "Is it OK if I go to camp? You said we would talk about it when I was done."

Charlotte knitted a few more stitches on the blanket she was making for Will, regret spinning through her at what she knew she had to tell her granddaughter. "I don't know if I can let you go, honey."

Emily frowned. "What do you mean?"

"I'll be busy with Hannah, bringing her back and forth to visit Frank in the hospital. I won't have time to do everything on the farm and in the house. I'm depending on you to help me."

Emily's mouth fell open, and her shoulders sagged. "Why do I have to help? Why can't the boys pitch in?"

"They're not nearly as capable as you are in the house. I mean, look what you accomplished tonight. Without any prodding you got supper going, cleaned the house, folded the laundry, and put it away. It was so wonderful to come home and find everything taken care of."

Emily leaned forward, her hands clasped together, her eyes bright. "I really, really want to go. I've never been to a camp before. I think it would be so much fun. There's canoeing and horseback riding and crafts and all kinds of things I don't know anything about."

The earnest tone of her granddaughter's voice was almost Charlotte's undoing. "I'm sorry, honey," she said, injecting as much sympathy as she could into her voice. "I'm really going to need you the next little while. There's no way I can do everything here and still take care of Hannah."

Emily pulled back and straightened, her features hardening. "That's not fair."

"What do you mean?"

"I did all that work so you'd let me go. If I had known that by doing you a favor I would have ended up stuck on the farm instead, I would've never done everything."

Just as Bob opened his mouth to reprimand her, Emily scrambled to her feet, ran down the hallway, and stormed up the stairs. At least she didn't slam the door to her bedroom, Charlotte thought thankfully.

She pressed her fingers to her temple, trying to ease away the headache. She had sincerely thought Emily had done what she did out of the goodness of her heart. To find out her granddaughter had had an ulterior motive hurt her.

"Did I make the right decision?" she asked Bob, needing to have her choice confirmed.

That was one of the other joys of raising teenagers: the second-guessing that twisted her in circles.

"Hannah needs you, and that's more important than Emily's summer entertainment." Bob leaned back in his recliner with another sigh. "Besides, pitching in a bit more wouldn't hurt Emily. She doesn't have a job yet so she may as well keep busy here."

Charlotte agreed, but at the same time she wished she could let her granddaughter attend camp. Just last month she'd had to deny her going to the prom. And now this.

She'd like to allow it for her granddaughter's sake, yes, but also for the peace of the household. Because a happy Emily was a happy household. If she couldn't go to this camp that she "really, really" wanted to attend, the whole household would suffer.

Charlotte settled back in her chair; to soothe herself, she picked up her knitting. Bill, Anna, and the children were coming on Sunday for dinner, and she had hoped to have the blanket ready by then. Maybe she could take it to the hospital tomorrow and work on it while Hannah visited with Frank.

She tried to push down the panic swirling in her mind at the thought of being gone all day tomorrow and all the things she needed to do.

Emily could help, she reminded herself. Christopher could help. In spite of Emily's obvious resentment, Charlotte knew her granddaughter would be obedient.

She also knew there would be a cost.

As she started knitting a new row, she thought of what Sam and Christopher had said about Troy calling so often, and more second thoughts assailed her.

Maybe it would be best if Emily and Troy had some time away from each other, but was that really a solution?

She needed Emily's help. Hannah's well-being was more important than Emily's going to camp.

She twisted the yarn around her needle, wishing she could make up her mind.

A few minutes later the phone rang. Charlotte didn't even bother to get up to answer it. With two teenagers and a young boy in the house, it seldom rang for her and Bob anymore.

A few minutes later, Emily trudged down the stairs, phone in hand. "Even though I'm not going to camp, is it okay if I go to Ashley's tomorrow? Sam said he would give me a ride."

"How long will you be there?"

Emily lifted her one shoulder in a negligent shrug. "I dunno. Couple of hours."

Charlotte glanced at Bob watching his television show. No help from that department.

"Okay. I'll need your help tomorrow afternoon though. We've got company coming on Sunday, and I'd like you to do some more baking Saturday afternoon."

"What do you want me to make?"

"A couple of pies for dessert and another banana bread."

Emily just nodded.

"So make sure—"

"That I'm back on time. I know."

"Okay then." Charlotte hoped her gentle smile would soothe her obviously frustrated granddaughter. "I'll be at the hospital with Hannah, so if you could be back by three o'clock, that should give you enough time to get the baking done before supper."

"Do I have to make supper too?"

Charlotte thought that might be asking a bit much, so she shook her head. "I'll think of something. Maybe I can pick up something at Mel's Place in town."

Emily didn't reply.

"So is that okay with you?" Charlotte pressed, requiring at least some acknowledgement.

"Sure. Okay." Emily's mouth barely moved as she spoke, as if each word was begrudgingly given.

Once again Charlotte held back a reprimand.

Choose the battles you want to fight.

The old advice was never more apt than when dealing with her grandchildren.

"Say hello to Ashley for me," Charlotte said, pointing at the phone Emily still held in her hand.

Emily hesitated and then gave Charlotte a begrudging smile. "I will. Thanks, Grandma."

When she was gone, Bob sighed. "Always some drama," he said, but his smile softened the comment.

"Keeps us young," Charlotte said returning his smile.

Chapter Three

There they go again.

Christopher stood in the driveway petting Toby as he watched Sam and Emily drive away, a cloud of dust billowing behind them.

Sam was going to work, Emily was visiting Ashley, and he was stuck here on the farm. He was tired of always being left behind. Normally he liked Saturdays on the farm, but it was summertime, and today, Saturday felt like Friday, which felt like Thursday during the school year.

Tomorrow his cousins, Jennifer and Madison, were coming after church and that would be fun; but that was tomorrow. Right now it was today, and today he didn't want to be by himself, especially if he couldn't play his Nintendo DS.

He sighed, and Toby pushed her wet nose against his hand. "I'm bored, and no one seems to care," he said, patting her head. "Except you."

He went to the house just as Grandma and Mrs. Carter came out.

"Christopher! Just who I was looking for," Grandma said with a voice that meant she had a job for him. "Emily didn't have time to vacuum the upstairs, so could you do that for me?"

Great. Now things were even worse. Now he had to do girl work because Emily got to go away for the day.

Not fair.

"All right." He let go another big sigh just to let Grandma know he was annoyed.

"I'll be with you in a minute," Grandma said to Mrs. Carter, and from the way she sounded, Christopher knew he was in trouble. Grandma waited until the car door closed and then turned to him. She was frowning.

Yup. Trouble for sure.

He made sure he didn't sigh this time.

"Christopher, I know you think this isn't fair," she said. "Maybe it isn't, but for the next few days I'm depending on you."

Christopher shoved his hands in his pockets and dug his toe in the dirt.

Grandma waited a minute, and Christopher knew she wanted him to answer.

"Yes, Grandma," he mumbled.

Grandma put her hand under his chin and tilted his face up to her. "Honey, I wish I didn't have to ask, but I do. Mrs. Carter is not feeling well, and she's worried about Mr. Carter. She needs me to help her. But the only way I can help her is to ask you, Sam, and Emily to do some more work."

"But Emily gets to go to Ashley's, and Sam is working all the time and hanging out with Arielle, and I won't be able to see him much before he starts college..." Christopher stopped. He didn't want to sound like a crybaby, but he was feeling a bit sorry for himself.

"Oh, honey." Grandma bent over and gave him a hug. "I understand, and I feel bad for you. But you'll probably be seeing more of Sam over this summer than you did when you were both in school." She stood up and stroked his head. "He'll be around to help you with the work."

Christopher nodded. He was sad about Sam going to college, but he hoped Grandma would feel sorry enough for him that she would tell him he could play on his DS.

"And another thing, Christopher..."

Grandma had turned on her serious voice, indicating more trouble.

"I don't want you to play your DS until your work is done, okay? I'm not here to keep an eye on you, so I'm counting on you to do what I say."

So much for that.

"Can I play when I'm done?"

"I'd prefer if you played outside."

"Okay." Maybe he could take his DS outside.

"And playing outside means leaving your DS behind in the house."

Christopher's mouth fell open, and he just stared at Grandma. How did she know?

Grandma just smiled at him, patted him on the shoulder again, and then walked to the car.

"Hannah and I will be back before supper," she said as she got into the car. "Be a good boy now."

Christopher gave a halfhearted wave as Grandma drove away. He didn't feel like a good boy. Didn't feel like *being* a good boy. Right now he wanted to throw something. But he wouldn't do it because someone would find out and he would just get into trouble again.

He walked back to the house and stomped up the stairs. At least no one could hear that, he thought with a bit of satisfaction. Then he turned on the vacuum cleaner and started working. Now he knew exactly what Cinderella felt like.

Cinderfella. That's what he should call himself.

Not fair.

"JUST DROP ME OFF HERE," Emily said, reaching into the back of the car for her backpack as Sam stopped at the intersection. "I can walk to Ashley's house."

"Are you sure?" Sam teased, glancing down the street, pretending to be amazed. "Must be at least two whole blocks."

Emily made a face at him. "I'm tougher than I look," she said as she hopped out of the car. "You'll pick me up at two thirty?"

"That's the plan."

Emily slammed the door shut and jogged away, her backpack and ponytail bouncing behind her.

Before pulling away, Sam pulled out his cell phone and entered Arielle's number. He hadn't had a chance to call her last night, and he planned to take her out tonight.

"Hey, Sam," she said, answering on the second ring, sounding breathless.

"Hey, yourself. What's up?"

"I'm at Jenny's Creamery."

"Good call. Why don't I meet you there?"

"Well, I'm working here now."

"What?"

"Yeah. I stopped in at the creamery this morning. It's *so* hot, and I needed an ice cream. One of Jenny's workers quit on her last night, and she needed extra help for the summer."

"But what about your day-care job?"

"Oh, I'm still doing that, but this way I can get extra money for college. She asked me to work a bunch of evenings as well."

"And Kepler's?"

"I'll squeeze that in when I can. I'm not getting lots of hours there anyway, so I'm sure I can figure something out."

"When do you start?" Sam asked, feeling an inkling of worry. Sounded like she would be busy today.

"I'm working right now. I won't be off until about nine o'clock tonight. Why do you want to know?"

"Well, it *is* a Saturday night, and I was kind of hoping we could do something together."

"I have to wait and see how I feel," Arielle said.

"What do you mean?" Sam's grip tightened on his cell phone. He wasn't so sure he liked the direction this conversation was going.

"I was thinking I might be kind of tired. It's really busy in here, and I'm still trying to get a handle on things."

"But you won't know how tired you'll be until you're done with work." Sam didn't want to sound angry, but he was starting to feel frustrated. For the entire two weeks before school was over, Arielle said she couldn't go out with him because she had to study. Then, when school was out, she said she was tired from all the studying. They'd had only a couple of dates together, and now she practically had three jobs.

Sam rubbed his forehead with his fingertips, trying to figure out how this would work. Come September, he and Arielle would go their separate ways. He was already trying to figure out how they would maintain a long-distance relationship and keep up their studies.

All this week, Sam had been making plans for things they could do together the rest of the summer so they could spend as much time together as possible. Kind of cement the relationship. He thought they'd have lots of time to hike, swim, hang out at the mall in Harding.

Now he would be stuck at home twiddling his thumbs while she worked literally day and night. He had to get some more hours at the airport.

"I've got to get going," Arielle was saying. "So I guess I'll see you tomorrow at church?"

"Yeah. I guess that's where we'll have to meet up."

"You sound a little miffed. Is everything OK?"

"Yeah. Everything is just peachy." Sam put his car in gear and started driving down the road. "I've got to get going. Good luck with the new job."

He snapped his phone shut before she could say goodbye or ask him what was so important. He felt like a bit of a jerk, but right now he was mad. Arielle was supposed to be his girlfriend, but he seemed to be working harder on the relationship than she was.

If it was like that now, what would it be like when they went to different colleges halfway across the state from each other?

Sam threw his phone down and hit the accelerator. The car fishtailed on the gravel, straightened itself, and then sped down the road. He was probably driving too fast, but right now he didn't care.

By the time he got to the Adams County Airport, he had settled down a bit. But he was still feeling frustrated and angry. Maybe it wasn't the best time to talk to his boss about getting more hours, but if he didn't do it now he knew he'd chicken out. He stopped by the board where the work schedule was posted. He had two hours on Monday, four on Wednesday, and four more on Friday. This was even worse than before.

Ed Haffner was sitting at his desk surrounded by grease-stained papers when Sam knocked at the door. He looked up from the calculator he'd been punching numbers into, and Sam wasn't encouraged by the frown on his boss's face.

Then the frown disappeared. "Hey, Sam. I didn't think you were working today."

"I'm not. I just stopped by to check my hours." Sam fidgeted, wondering how to go about this.

Ed gave him an encouraging smile. "Is there anything you need, Sam?"

"Actually. Yeah. I just looked at the work schedule, and, well, I noticed I have even fewer hours than last week."

Ed nodded. "I know. I'm really sorry."

"See, here's the thing: I was hoping I could get some more hours in. I'm going to college this fall, and I could use the extra money."

Ed sat back in his chair, his arms crossed over his stained coveralls, and slowly shook his head. "I'm really sorry, Sam. I just hired a new guy. He's got two kids and is a pretty decent mechanic. He'll need all the hours he can get."

"So you can't find a way to get me a few more?" Sam asked, feeling like a beggar.

"I've got enough other guys working here who are supporting families. They're my first priority."

"Okay. I understand." Sam wished he could be a bit more sincere about his understanding. Truth was, he really could use the extra hours too. He wasn't supporting a family, but he needed the money for college. Of course that was a bit selfish.

"So we'll see you next week then?" Ed said, giving Sam an encouraging smile.

"Yeah. Sure." Sam left, feeling even lower than when he got there. Wasn't his life just dandy? His girlfriend was avoiding him and holding down three jobs, and his hours had been cut on the single job he had, which meant he wouldn't get more money, which meant if even the smallest thing went wrong with his car, he was out of luck.

He got into the Datsun and cranked up the radio, ignoring the crackling from the poor reception. If he were in San Diego...

Sam held that thought a moment and then discarded it.

If he were still in San Diego he might not have this car. It was only thanks to Uncle Pete and Grandpa helping him fix it that he could afford to keep it on the road. If he were in San Diego, he might not even be able to find a part-time job.

So, as Grandma would say, he had to count his blessings. Trouble was, there didn't seem to be a ton of them today.

He kept on driving, heading into town. Maybe Jake or Paul was working at the store. He could arrange to hook up with them after work. Maybe he could do what Arielle had done. Find another job. Wouldn't that be just peachy?

He pushed open the door of the video store and almost bumped into Nicole Evans.

"Hey, Sam," she said, flicking her hair over her shoulder. "Are you glad school's over too?"

"Yeah. Enjoying the break from school."

She flashed him a smile. "Me too. You and Arielle have plans for the summer?"

"Yeah. Of course." Sam was never sure whether he liked Nicole or not. Sure she was cute and all, and sometimes she seemed interested in him, but the girl was always on Emily's case.

And getting on Emily's case was his job, thank you very much.

"Well . . . see ya," she said, flashing him another smile as she tossed her hair over her other shoulder. Her purple T-shirt and funky pants reminded him of the way Emily dressed.

If Sam didn't know that Nicole couldn't stand Emily, he'd say for sure she was trying to copy his sister.

"Yeah. See ya around," he echoed, stepping through the door of the video store only to be greeted by the sound of an explosion and a burst of dramatic music.

Jake had his favorite movie playing on the screen again.

One of the perks of working in the video store, he always told Sam. But his friend wasn't behind the counter.

Sam glanced around the store, his eyes flicking past the movies displayed along the outer wall and the shelves of older DVDs filling the rest of the store.

The music grew even louder, followed by another explosion, and right then Jake stuck his head over the top of a shelf in the center of the store. He pushed his dark hair back from his face.

"Aren't you sick of this movie yet?" Sam called out.

"Maybe after the twentieth time I might be." Jake flashed him a grin and then sauntered around the shelves in that loose-limbed walk of his. "What brings you to town?"

Boredom.

"Actually I'm looking for a job. Is the store hiring?"

"Nah, man. Not these days. You quit your airport job?"

Sam shook his head. "Still working there, but I'm just not getting enough hours. I'm trying to get money together for college, and I'm barely getting enough time to keep gas in my car."

Jake picked up a DVD and moved it to another spot. "That sucks. Whatcha gonna do?"

"Like I said, look for another job."

"You and Arielle goin' out tonight?"

"Nah. She just got a job working at Jenny's."

"Scooped you on that job, did she?" Jake punched his shoulder.

"I just found out this afternoon." Sam absently flicked through the DVDs in the half-price bin. "What are you and Paul doing tonight? You want to meet up at the school? We could work on a few rails. I haven't been on my skateboard since school got out."

"Nah. Can't." Jake picked up another DVD. "Gotta work."

Which made Sam feel even more like a loser. "Sure. Of course. Well, see ya around."

"You can hang here for a while if you want."

Sam glanced up at the movie. The explosions had quit, and dust was settling on the movie-set city. The hero was looking around, a puzzled expression on his face.

"Could my day get any worse than this?" Sam said at exactly the same time as the hero did. Then he looked at Jake. "I've seen this movie seven times too many."

"Dude, you can never see this movie too many times. That's like saying you can have too many burgers."

Sam punched his friend on the shoulder and then left the store, heading to his car.

Partway down the sidewalk, he stopped and glanced down Main Street. He was here now, no harm in going around to some of the places, see if they were hiring.

The pharmacy wasn't hiring. Neither was the *Bedford Leader*. Ditto Herko's Grocery. He decided to give Jenny's Creamery and his Aunt Rosemary's shop, Fabrics and Fun, a pass. He worked his way up and down Main Street.

Two hours later he was driving home, his mood even worse than before. No offers. No bites. No nothing.

Looked like he was stuck working at the airport and making just enough to put new tires on his car before he left for college.

"AND WE PRAY that You will grant healing to our brother Frank Carter. Hold him in Your hands. Be with Hannah. Give her strength to deal with whatever comes her way. Amen."

Pastor Evans waited a moment, adjusted his glasses on his face and then rose to his feet, his knees creaking as he unfolded his narrow frame from the chair. He looked from Frank to Hannah, who still sat with her hands twisted on her lap.

Charlotte waited for her to say some word of thanks to Pastor Evans, but she just stared at Frank, who was sleeping, his heavy breathing mingling with the beeping of the monitors surrounding his bed.

Charlotte gave Pastor Evans a quick smile. "Thank you so much for coming. I know Saturday is usually your day off," she said quietly as they walked to the door.

"I came as soon as I heard. And I often work on my sermon on Saturday anyhow." He shifted his Bible from one hand to the other. "Hannah seems tired."

"She is." Charlotte glanced back at her friend, concern filling her. "Trouble is, she's not feeling well herself."

"I'm sure this has been quite a blow for her." Pastor Evans scratched the side of his nose. "It's a blessing you can be with her."

Charlotte didn't feel like much of a blessing. She found herself growing increasingly weary with each passing hour.

"I do what I can," she said.

Pastor Evans left, and Charlotte returned to her friend.

"That was nice of Pastor Evans to come," Charlotte said, standing beside Hannah's chair.

"It was." Hannah closed her eyes, rubbing her forehead with her fingers. "I sure wish the doctor would come and tell us what's up," she continued, twisting the cuffs of her sweatshirt. She wore a purple sweatshirt today with a butterfly appliqué on the front.

"The nurse said he would be here soon," Charlotte assured her, patting her friend's hand.

I guess we're getting old, she thought, comparing her hands and Hannah's. Charlotte's hands held a few more brown age spots, but Hannah wasn't too far behind.

When did this happen? When did their smooth hands get that crepey skin she remembered as so normal on her mother's hands? When did those laugh lines around their mouths and eyes become permanently etched in?

It seemed like only a short time ago that she and Hannah were young brides, making big plans. They were going to be the perfect wives, the best mothers.

Hannah and Frank never had children, and Charlotte's only daughter ran away at age eighteen.

Life happened to them while they were making other plans, as the saying went.

"Do you think they'll have to do surgery?" Hannah asked.

"I have no idea, Hannah," Charlotte answered. "We'll just have to wait and see. I know that's easier said than done."

"I'm keeping you away from your family."

"My family will manage just fine without me," Charlotte said. "You don't have to worry about the kids. Besides, Emily is helping out."

Hannah gave Charlotte a wistful smile. "You are so blessed."

Charlotte wondered if Hannah would have thought that if she had seen Emily's face last night.

A couple of nurses passed by in the hallway, laughing at a shared joke. Charlotte was reminded that life carried on in spite of the drama going on in Frank's hospital room.

"Mrs. Carter?"

Both women spun around to see a doctor standing behind them, his hands tucked in the pockets of an immaculate white lab coat. His short dark hair was combed back from his face, his goatee expertly trimmed. He looked capable, in charge—and very, very young.

"My name is Dr. West. I'd like to give you an update on your husband," he said. "I'm sorry I wasn't here yesterday when you came in."

"Are you his doctor?" Hannah asked.

"I'm the resident cardiologist." Dr. West spoke quietly, as if to soften what he was about to say. "Has anyone spoken to you about your husband's condition?"

Hannah shook her head. "Not really. All I've been told is that he had a heart attack and that he might need bypass surgery."

"That's correct." The doctor nodded gently, but Charlotte had the feeling something more was coming. "Your husband will be needing surgery as soon as possible," Dr. West said. "We will be running more tests on him, and then we hope to book him into the OR this afternoon."

"That soon?" Charlotte asked the question she knew Hannah did not dare voice.

"The sooner the better where these things are concerned," the doctor responded.

Hannah squeezed Charlotte's hand even tighter. "What does the surgery entail?"

The doctor gave her a careful smile. "It's not an uncommon procedure." He slipped his hands out of his pockets and began rocking on his heels. "I'd like to back up so you understand. The reason Mr. Carter had a heart attack was that his coronary arteries are blocked with plaque, restricting the flow of blood to his heart. We need to go past those blocked blood vessels."

"So how do you do that?" Charlotte asked.

"What we do is harvest a healthy blood vessel from another part of his body and graft it above and below the blocked portion of his artery. Hence the name *bypass*."

Charlotte tried to absorb this information. "That sounds fairly extensive."

Dr. West glanced from Hannah to Charlotte, as if he had more to say and was testing their reaction.

"Actually, we'll probably have to do a double bypass. Two of his arteries are blocked." Dr. West looked past them to Frank, still sleeping. "Try not to worry. We do this all the time."

"How long will he have to be in the hospital?" Hannah managed to ask.

"Once the surgery is performed, there will be the usual postoperative care. He'll spend some time in the cardiac care unit." Dr. West lifted his shoulders in a careful shrug. "The first twenty-four hours after surgery are critical. Then we have to wait to see how the grafts take, how he recuperates from surgery. I'm guessing he'll need at least four days there, maybe more."

"And once he's home?"

"Wound care. Lifestyle changes."

In the silence that followed Dr. West's pronouncement, Charlotte noticed a lab technician pushing a rattling cart down the hallway. The noise grated on Charlotte's nerves as she tried to absorb what Dr. West was saying.

"As in . . . ," Charlotte asked.

"The usual diet changes: cut out fat and caffeine, lower his sodium intake. And once he's recuperated enough, he'll need to start a program of regular exercise, starting mildly at first." The doctor gave them another smile. "None of this is too onerous, and we'll be having a dietitian cover the changes he'll have to make. I wanted to give you the news up front so you wouldn't have any unexpected shocks."

It seemed everything over the past twenty-four hours had been an unexpected shock, Charlotte thought. She glanced at Hannah, who stood by Frank, holding his hand. She didn't say anything, but Charlotte could easily read the distress on her face.

"Thanks for the information." She didn't know what else to say.

Dr. West then walked over to Frank, glanced at his chart, and then checked his IV and blood pressure monitors and all the other beeping and squealing machines attached to Frank. "Everything seems to be OK so far. Do you have any other questions?"

Charlotte waited, but Hannah said nothing.

Dr. West smoothed his hand over his goatee as he glanced from Hannah to Frank, but still Hannah was quiet.

"He's doing well, all things considered," Dr. West said. "There are risks, of course, but this surgery has a very high success rate. We'll do our best, and if everything goes well, he'll be fine."

Charlotte suspected he was trying to reassure Hannah, but from the look on her friend's face, Charlotte could see she was anything but reassured.

"Thanks for your time," Charlotte said, taking charge of the situation. "If we have any questions, we'll write them down."

"Excellent." He waited a beat and then turned and walked away, the soft soles of his shoes squeaking faintly on the polished floor.

Hannah sank back into the chair behind her, her hand trembling as she placed it on her own heart.

"Oh, Charlotte. This is even worse than I thought."

Charlotte sat down beside her friend, slipping her arm around Hannah's shoulders. "The doctor seemed fairly confident."

"Did you hear what he was saying? Grafting arteries and cutting out veins." She shook her head as if trying to process the information. "I can't go back to my house now," Hannah said. "I'll be thinking about Frank constantly."

"Don't worry about that. As long as you need to, you will be staying at our place. I don't want you to be alone."

Hannah gave Charlotte a wavery smile, her eyes glistening with tears. "You are a dear friend. I don't know what I would do without you. Are you sure it's OK that I stay at your place? Are you sure I won't be in the way? Will I keep you from your work?"

"I wouldn't offer if I didn't mean it. As for my work, I have a very capable granddaughter." Charlotte squeezed Hannah's hand, thankful she had not agreed to let Emily go to camp. In the next couple of weeks she would need her granddaughter more than ever.

"Will you stay with me today?" Hannah asked.

Charlotte gave her a tender smile. "Of course. I'll be here as long as you need me."

The rest of the morning passed in a blur of tests and consultations between doctors. Charlotte had called Bob to let him know about the surgery but didn't expect that he would be coming to the hospital.

When they wheeled Frank out of the ICU to the operating room, a net covering his hair, nurses and orderlies taking care of the paraphernalia attached to him, fear clutched at Charlotte.

This was it. No return.

They paused, allowing Hannah to kiss Frank; the sight of her friend, bent over her husband to say good-bye, created a heartache in Charlotte that only another wife could understand.

Then, with a swish of wheels and closing doors, he was gone.

Hannah blinked, looking dazed. Charlotte led her to a waiting room, sat her in a chair, and sat down beside her.

They had prayed, had shed a few tears. Now all they could do was wait.

Chapter Four

Christopher sat with his elbows on his knees, his chin in his hand as he stared out over the quiet farmyard. Even though it was getting close to supper, the day was still hot.

A few flies buzzed overhead, and in the distance he heard the clank of tools coming from the shed where Uncle Pete and Grandpa were still working.

The last time he went into the house, the phone rang. It was Grandma telling him that Mr. Carter had to have surgery right away. Whatever that meant. Then she told him to make sure he didn't play on the computer.

But how would Grandma know if he did or not?

So he'd gone back outside and tried to catch Magic, his 4-H lamb. It took awhile and when he finally did, the lamb was being stubborn and wouldn't follow very well.

He had already vacuumed the upstairs and cleaned up his bedroom, like Grandma asked him; he'd talked to the horses and made sure Trudy was fed. He'd checked the chickens and gathered eggs, and now he was bored, bored, bored.

Uncle Pete always said there were no boring things, only boring people. But Uncle Pete was wrong. Being left alone on the farm on a Saturday was boring.

Toby came up to him and nudged his elbow with her long, pointy nose. Christopher patted her absently on the head. Toby whined, like she wanted to do something. Christopher felt a bit sorry for her. He knew she wanted to go for a walk, but the heat made him feel lazy.

"Guess we could go see what Uncle Pete and Grandpa are doing," he said to Toby, pushing himself up to his feet.

He walked over to the tractor shed where Uncle Pete and Grandpa were working.

"I told you it won't fit without the proper O-ring," he heard Uncle Pete saying in a loud voice.

"Then you should have *given* me the proper O-ring," Grandpa snapped back.

Guess he wasn't going in there. They didn't sound very happy.

A squirrel ran down a tree close to the shed, saw Toby, and then scooted off into the grass behind the shed. Toby ran after her.

"Get back here, Toby," Christopher called, chasing after the dog. Her trail led him by a bunch of stuff behind the toolshed, all grown over with grass. Behind that was a little shed with a sagging roof and an old truck next to it. When he first came here, both Uncle Pete and Grandpa had told him he was never, ever to play behind the toolshed or in the old shed with the sagging roof. They were very firm about it.

And he never did.

But if it was that dangerous, then Toby shouldn't be there either.

He called Toby, but she didn't answer. Then he heard a yelp, like she was hurt.

Should he follow her?

He looked over at the tall grass and the pieces of equipment sticking out above it; then he looked back at the old shed.

He was older and bigger now. If he was big enough to do vacuuming, he was big enough to go where he hadn't been allowed to go before.

He walked behind the toolshed, keeping an eye out for Uncle Pete or Grandpa. He heard them still arguing inside. He glanced over his shoulder one more time, feeling a bit excited and scared at the same time.

He walked carefully through the tall grass. It was even thicker than when he first came here. Then his foot hit something hard, hidden in the grass, and he just about tripped.

He bent over and tugged at the waist-high grass, brushing some of it aside and pulling some up by the roots as he worked his way along the thing, whatever it was. A few minutes later his work revealed a long wooden bar with two rounded bars attached to it. The rounded bars had metal caps on the ends, and attached to the metal caps were large loops. He couldn't figure out what it was, but it looked old.

There had to be other things hidden in the grass. Excited

with this find, he started exploring further. The old shed, the one Grandpa had always warned him away from, made him suddenly want to go inside.

Maybe it was dangerous, but he was a big kid now, he figured. He could go in there. Besides, who knew what other things he would find?

The inside of the building was dark and smelled funny, like old metal and dust. Christopher had to blink a moment to get used to the gloom, and when he did, his heart jumped a little.

The roof of the little shed sagged inward, and stripes of light shone through spots where parts of the roof no longer met. Now he understood why Grandpa didn't like him going in here. The roof looked so flimsy, Christopher suspected a summer breeze could push it down into the building.

As he got used to the gloom, he saw Toby's tail, and then on the ground near Toby he saw a funny-looking thing. It had what looked like a big metal cup on the top and two round plates about four inches across attached to a handle. Looked kind of like a meat grinder, but he knew it wasn't that.

On the ground beside it he saw a long wooden handle. He picked it up, and his heart jumped when only part of it came up off the ground. Then he realized it was hinged in the middle with leather straps.

This was old stuff, he realized, remembering some of the things they had learned in school when they talked about pioneers. He knew Grandma and Grandpa weren't pioneers, but Grandpa's dad had grown up on this farm. Maybe this stuff belonged to him.

Growing more and more excited, he climbed over an old bed and mattress. He saw cardboard boxes with the sides falling away and wooden boxes and crates.

He had found a treasure! He wished his friend Dylan was here to see this. He would know what to do with it.

Maybe Uncle Pete would help him.

As soon as the thought came into his mind, he pushed it away. Uncle Pete was too busy with the farm, and now that he was married, he wasn't around much anymore in the evenings.

Christopher sighed as he looked around. At least now he had something to do. Though what he would do with all this stuff, he wasn't sure. For now though, he had to try to figure out what all of it was. Looked like he'd have to go on the computer after all. But how would he remember what everything looked like?

He took one more look around and then had a great idea. He could take pictures of the stuff with the camera their dad had gotten Emily for Christmas. One way or another, he would figure out what all this stuff was, where it had come from, and what he could do with it. He turned and crawled over some stuff to get out. Then he felt a tug, heard a rip, and stopped. He twisted his leg and sighed. Another pair of pants ripped on the knee. Grandma would not be happy.

His other favorite pants were still in her mending basket waiting to be patched. Guess Grandma had another job to do.

CHARLOTTE PULLED UP to the house, weariness clawing at her limbs. The last time she'd been this tired was after she'd helped Anna through labor last December, but she didn't dare show it. Right now her focus was Hannah. She turned to her friend and forced a smile. "Let's go inside, and I'll get us some iced tea."

Hannah shook her head. "You know, I think I should just go home. You've got enough going on, what with your company coming tomorrow."

Charlotte quelled a moment of panic at the thought of Bill and Anna's visit, but she had asked Emily to do some baking, so at least that was done. She could have canceled, but she knew how much Bill and Anna's girls loved coming to the farm. Besides, she hadn't seen baby Will for a few weeks and missed him.

"You know you were invited to come and spend the day with us anyway, so that's no reason not to be here. Besides, Emily will be helping me," she added.

"As long as it's not too much trouble," Hannah insisted with a tiny show of her previous backbone. Then she slowly got out of the car.

Charlotte watched her with some concern. It seemed as if her friend had aged ten years in the past two days. First there was Frank's heart attack and then the news of how serious it was, followed by his surgery this afternoon. It was enough to knock anyone back on her heels.

After Frank's surgery had been successfully completed and he was stabilized, the nurses suggested that Hannah head home. They didn't allow visitors in the cardiac care unit for more than a few minutes at a time and since he was still heavily sedated, it didn't make much sense for Hannah to stay any longer since she herself wasn't feeling well.

It had been a long drive home, though, and Charlotte realized she would have to stay strong for her friend. Hannah had always done so much for her, being a support was the very least she could do right now.

Charlotte sent up a prayer for strength, pasted a smile on her face, and walked with Hannah up to the house. As she opened the door she frowned. It was strangely quiet.

She glanced at her watch. Six thirty. Supper should have been going already. She'd left instructions for Emily on the phone.

But obviously Emily wasn't here. Nor was Christopher.

She looked back over her shoulder and realized Sam's car wasn't back yet.

What were those kids thinking?

Of course, that was the trouble. They didn't always think. She needed them now. Didn't they understand that?

She forced herself not to march angrily into the kitchen. She had too much to do and not enough time to do it, and she didn't want her friend Hannah to see her frustration.

"Why don't you sit down and I'll get you that iced tea I promised," she said quietly.

"That would be so nice." Hannah wilted into a nearby chair, resting her face on her upturned palm. "I don't know what I would do without you," she said. "You are a dear friend and so patient."

Charlotte didn't feel as if she deserved the praise right now.

Emily would simply have to work after supper to get the baking done, she thought as she moved around the kitchen. Thank goodness school was out so she wouldn't have the excuse of homework.

She found a few cookies in the jar and glanced into the refrigerator, glad to see that the pitcher of iced tea she had made last night was still half full.

Just as she took the pitcher out, the sound of a car made her look up. But it wasn't Sam who came driving into the yard.

It was Mel.

What was she doing here?

Melody Givens got out of her car, carrying a couple of stacked boxes she secured with her chin. Her hair was still covered with a hairnet, and a stained apron swaddled her ample figure.

Had she come directly from work? And if so, why?

Then Charlotte saw Emily behind Mel, carrying a larger box but walking a bit more slowly. Why was Emily with Mel? What were they bringing here?

Charlotte met them at the doorway of the porch. "Melody, come in. This is a pleasant surprise." She glanced past Melody at Emily, who had a pained look on her face.

Melody grinned and stepped inside. "That's always good to hear. I'd hate to be an unpleasant surprise, though maybe what I've got might be."

"Hannah and I are having some iced tea in the kitchen. Would you like to join us?" Charlotte asked.

"Sounds wonderful, but no thanks. I just stopped by to bring Emily home and make a delivery. Emily told me what happened to Frank and that Hannah is staying with you." Melody set the boxes she carried on the freezer in the porch.

"I'm sorry I didn't come sooner, Grandma. I know I said I would, but Sam didn't come and pick me up." Emily sounded so worried that Charlotte's momentary pique with her faded like frost in the sun.

"Honey, that's OK—"

"So Ashley called her mom, and she came home and brought some stuff from the cafe because I told Ashley I had to be home in time to get some baking done." Emily's words came out in a rush, and Charlotte felt bad for the pressure the poor girl had been under.

Pressure she had placed on her granddaughter's shoulders by her insistence that she be back on time.

"It's okay, honey. It's not your fault." She would have a few words with Sam when he finally came rolling in.

"So here's the stuff. I brought you a batch of muffins, some cookies, and a couple of pies," Melody said. "Hope that works out for you."

"More than—"

"Emily has a pot of soup and some buns in her treasure box," Melody continued, brushing a strand of hair away from her face. "So you shouldn't starve." She laughed at her own joke.

"I can't thank you enough."

"Well, then don't bother starting." Melody grew serious. "I know how much I appreciated all the help I got from you and the people in the community when I was recuperating from my cancer surgery. So I wanted to help you and Hannah—and help you help Hannah, if you get my drift."

Melody's last statement was delivered with her signature smile followed by a quick wink, easing away the seriousness of the moment.

"I get your drift, and thank you so much." Charlotte looked over the boxes with their tantalizing smells. "You are a lifesaver."

"I suspect Emily feels the same. Poor girl was in a bit of a frazzle trying to figure out how to get home on time to get her baking done." Melody patted Emily on the shoulder. "I helped her figure it out, and now I hope everything's okay."

Melody's remark was a subtle way of helping Charlotte forgive her granddaughter.

"Everything is just fine." Charlotte smiled at Emily. "Why don't you bring the boxes in the house, honey, and we can figure out what to do with Mel's generous donation."

Emily nodded, obviously pleased that all was well. She picked up her box again and headed into the kitchen.

"Now I gotta make like a banana and split," Mel said. "I have to make sure Ginny isn't putting too much salt in the soup or forgetting sugar in the pie." Mel tossed off a wave and opened the door. "Say hi to Hannah for me. I gotta run."

With a swish of her apron, Mel was out the door and down the driveway.

"Isn't this great?" Emily was saying as she picked up the last boxes. "I'm so sorry I didn't come sooner. But Sam wasn't answering his cell and I didn't know when he was coming."

Charlotte pushed aside her increasing anger with her grandson and gave Emily a quick smile. "Everything worked out just fine, my dear. I'm just glad you're home safely. Now let's go have some iced tea and enjoy some of the goodies you brought."

She knew she would have to deal with Sam when he came home and also find the energy to support her friend and plan a menu for tomorrow.

Chapter Five

"Hello, the house," Pete called out as the porch door slammed behind him. "I smell good food."

"Just the thing you should be smelling on a Sunday after church," Charlotte said over her shoulder as she gave the soup another stir. "Hello, Dana. You're looking lovely."

Dana wore an apple-green linen sheath with a green-and-purple scarf arranged artfully over her shoulders. Marriage agreed with her, Charlotte thought. Her eyes shone, and every time Charlotte saw her she was smiling.

"Thank you. I'm glad to be here."

Everything was ready for her company. Charlotte had driven Hannah to the hospital early this morning so she could see Frank. Hannah had assured her that she was fine spending some time alone with Frank while Charlotte went to church and prepared for the family lunch. She would get a ride back to Heather Creek Farm with Frank's sister and then would return to the hospital later that day with Charlotte and Bob.

"I didn't think Pastor Evans would ever be done preaching at us this morning," Pete grumbled. As he slipped off his jacket Charlotte was pleased to see that Pete wore a light blue shirt that set off the blue of his eyes, and a gray-and-black-striped tie.

"You clean up real nice," Charlotte said, adding a smile so he knew she was kidding him.

"Not quite as nice as my wife," Pete said, pulling Dana close to him. "Doesn't she look beautiful?"

"She looks beautiful, as always," Charlotte said, smiling at her son's obvious pride.

"Do you want some coffee or tea while we wait for the rest of the gang? They should be here any minute." Charlotte rubbed her forehead, trying to ease away the headache that had been hovering there all morning.

"I hope they show up soon. I'm starving," Pete said.

"It can't be because you didn't eat any breakfast," Dana said with a chuckle. She turned to Charlotte. "I never realized how much this man can put away. I wish someone would've warned me."

"I tried," Charlotte said, smiling. "So, Dana, are you as glad to be done with school as the kids seem to be?"

"She's been complaining the past week about not knowing how to keep herself busy this summer," Pete said, giving his young wife a one-armed hug. "I told her to save her energy for the new house."

"Well, I've got everything picked out already," Dana said, leaning against Pete. "There's not much to do until the electricians are done. Then I can call the drywallers to come in."

"That's my organized wife," Pete said, pride in his voice. "She's almost as organized as you, Ma."

"That's not saying much these days."

"Why do you say that?" Dana asked. "Is it because of Mr. Carter's heart attack? I'm sure having something like that happen to such a close friend must be disorienting."

Dana's astuteness comforted Charlotte. She gave Dana a smile, once again thankful for this lovely woman's presence in their lives. It was as if she had truly gained a daughter when Pete married her.

"Actually, yes. The past two days have been a whirlwind, and I feel like I'm just running around in circles trying to get everything done that I'm supposed to."

"By the way, how is Frank?"

"He had a double bypass yesterday and is recuperating." Speaking the words now made Charlotte even more uncomfortable than she'd been when Dr. West had made his pronouncement. "Hannah will be staying here with us so I can drive her back and forth to the hospital to visit him until he's ready to go home." Charlotte sighed. "She's with him now but should be back shortly to rest before we go back for visiting hours this evening. She didn't sleep well last night."

Charlotte had had a hard time sleeping herself. Thoughts of what Frank had been through had raced around her mind and filled her night with restlessness.

"I'm sorry to hear that." Pete lowered his voice. He waited a moment; then he wandered into the family room, greeted his father, and dropped into a chair beside Bob.

"Where are the kids?" Dana asked.

"Sam is upstairs talking to Arielle on the phone. Christopher is probably playing with his Nintendo DS in the hayloft now that Sam bought him some new batteries."

"And Emily?" Dana asked.

Charlotte sighed and glanced behind her, just in case Emily decided to make an appearance. Though she had thought they had made their peace yesterday, this morning Emily was out of sorts. All during church she had sulked in the pew and wouldn't sing along with the songs. "She's angry with me so she's moping upstairs."

"What is she upset about?"

"I told her she couldn't go to summer camp with Ashley. The campers are leaving tomorrow, and this morning Emily found out that Nicole Evans is also going and, obviously she isn't."

"I'm sure that didn't sit well," Dana said with a sigh. As a high school teacher, Dana was well aware of the intricacies and complications in the relationships of her students in general, and in Nicole and Emily's in particular. "Why can't you let her go?"

"I need her here on the farm. Especially now that Hannah is staying with us and needs me to drive her to the hospital."

"What does Emily need to do?"

"Clean the house. Weed the garden. Stay caught up on laundry. Help make supper. Make sure Christopher does his chores with the chickens, the cat, Toby, and his 4-H lamb. I'll do what I can, and I know it's a lot to ask of a teenager, but for the next little while, Hannah will need me, so I'm depending on Emily." A tiny wave of uncertainty lapped at her mind.

Emily was capable, of that she was certain. But willing? Especially knowing that her friend was at camp doing all kinds of fun things? Charlotte could already envision many confrontations ahead.

Dana leaned back against the counter, eating a cookie she had taken from the cookie jar. "I could do what needs to be done," she said quietly. "If Emily really wants to go to camp."

"But—"

"I'm a farmer's wife now," Dana said, licking a cookie crumb off her thumb. "It's time I took over some extra responsibilities. Pete and Christopher can help me, show me what I need to know."

Charlotte bit her lip as she considered her daughter-in-law's offer.

"I hope I'm not overstepping any boundaries here as far as Emily is concerned, but..." Dana let the rest of the sentence slide off unsaid.

"You're her aunt now. You can express your concerns," Charlotte said, curious as to what Dana was going to say.

"Okay, here it is: I think it might be a good idea for Emily to be away from Troy for a while." Dana brushed a tiny crumb off the front of her dress. "They're still young, and I know Troy is pretty crazy about her. I know he's proving himself to be a good kid, but a little time apart wouldn't be a bad thing for them." Charlotte considered this information. If anyone knew what was going on with Troy and Emily, it would be Dana, who had seen them at school every day.

Charlotte rubbed her forehead yet again, still unsure of what to do. "I'm not sure I want to put all this on your shoulders though."

"You were going to put it on Emily's," Dana reminded her with a twinkle in her eye.

"Emily has been on the farm for two years now. She knows what to do."

"And Emily will be moving away someday whereas I hope to be here as long as you've been," Dana added. "It's time I learn the ropes."

"It's great that you want to pitch in . . ." Charlotte still felt torn.

"I think it could work," Dana said. "At least consider it. Besides, Sam can show me what to do. He has time."

That was true enough. Yesterday Sam came home complaining he couldn't get more hours working at the airport, nor could he find another job anywhere in town. Once Charlotte found out what had kept him from picking Emily up on time, she had gone a bit easier on him, but she was still frustrated with him.

"Please, Charlotte," Dana continued. "I wouldn't offer if I weren't willing." She flashed Charlotte a reassuring smile. "Besides, as I said to Pete, I need something constructive to do for the next month while I wait for the next phase of the house."

"Okay then." Another burden had been eased off her

mind. "You're about to make one grumpy teenage girl very happy. Why don't you go and tell her? She'll be glad to see you anyhow."

"I love being the bearer of good news," Dana said, popping the last bit of cookie in her mouth.

Just as Charlotte watched Dana go find Emily, the porch door flew open, twanging on its spring. "Hey, Grandma! We're here," a young girl's voice called out.

Jennifer burst into the kitchen, silk ribbon askew in her dark hair, face flushed and enhanced with a triumphant grin. She adjusted her dress and bent over to pull up her white socks, which already held a liberal streak of dirt, and then she grinned up at Charlotte. "You don't have to wait anymore."

"That's wonderful to know," Charlotte said, her mood instantly elevating.

"And I beat Madison, even though I'm only six." Jennifer dropped into a nearby chair, catching her breath.

"You cheated," Madison called out from the porch. Jennifer's older sister entered, looking prim and tidy, her hair neatly tied up in her ribbon and her socks still pulled up. "I didn't think you were going to run."

Jennifer rolled her eyes in her best cousin-Emily imitation. "Well, it was a race, silly. Of course I was going to run."

"Mommy says you're not supposed to run in your Sunday clothes." Madison sniffed, mustering all the dignity available to an eight-year-old girl.

"Hey, guys, you're here," Emily said as she descended

the stairs, her voice joyous. Obviously Dana had already told her the good news about going to camp.

Jennifer jumped off the chair and barreled down the hall to Emily, who caught her with a grunt.

"You're running again," Madison accused, following at a more sedate pace.

"Sorry we're late," Bill said, his voice booming into the house.

Anna entered behind Bill, setting baby Will's car seat on the floor.

"Is he awake?" Charlotte asked, hurrying over to see her youngest grandchild.

As soon as Charlotte bent over the car seat, Will flashed a toothless grin at her, his eyes as bright as marbles. He waved his arms and kicked his feet, gurgling his pleasure.

"I can't believe he's in such a good mood," Bill said. "I thought your pastor would never quit talking."

Charlotte stifled her displeasure with her older son's comment.

"Bill, Pastor Evans is one of the best pastors we've ever had. Did you know that Frank had his heart attack on Friday, and Pastor Evans was up in Harding visiting him Saturday morning?" Charlotte said, struggling to keep the prim note out of her voice.

"I know he's a good pastor, Mother," Bill said in the placating tone he'd perfected during his legal career, "but you have to admit, he does like to talk."

Anna's greeting spared Charlotte from replying to Bill's comment.

"Hello, Mother," Anna said quietly, as always the picture of elegance and composure. Her dark hair hung in glistening waves to her shoulders, and her eyebrows were perfectly plucked and outlined. Her flawless makeup and her powder-blue suit with its elbow-length sleeves, cowl neck, and pencil skirt reminded Charlotte of a young Jacqueline Kennedy. All Anna was missing was a pillbox hat.

Anna leaned over and kissed Charlotte on the cheek. "Hello, Anna." Charlotte smiled at her daughter-in-law.

Anna and Charlotte had shared an awkward relationship, but ever since Charlotte had coached her daughter-in-law through most of Will's delivery, the relationship had shifted. Charlotte had seen Anna at her most vulnerable, and now Anna could, on occasion, drop her guard and show a much warmer side.

"How are you doing?" Anna asked, allowing a tiny frown to mar the perfection of her forehead. "You look absolutely wrung out."

Warmer, yes. But still blunt.

"I'm tired," Charlotte agreed, unbuckling Will from his car seat. "Since Frank's heart attack and surgery, I've been helping Hannah."

"I was so sorry to hear about that," Anna said, taking a cloth and wiping a silvery line of drool from the corner of Will's mouth. She looked like she was about to say more but then glanced over Charlotte's shoulder and frowned again.

"Emily, you don't have to humor Jennifer's every whim."

Charlotte, holding Will close to her now, turned to see Emily giving Jennifer a piggyback ride, bouncing her up and down. The grin on Emily's face was worth every second thought Charlotte had had about letting her go to summer camp.

"Auntie Dana, you don't have to give me a piggyback ride," Madison reassured her aunt, holding Dana's hand. "Mommy said I'm supposed to be a little lady."

"And you're doing a great job," Dana said, suppressing a smile.

Sam joined them, obviously finished talking to Arielle. Christopher came in as well.

As everyone gathered around the table, Bob looked around, smiling. "Every time we get together, it seems we gain a few more family members," he said with a smile.

As she looked around the table, Charlotte felt uneasy. The light glinting off Bob's glasses, his scalp shining through his thinning hair—both served to remind her that he was getting older.

We both are, she thought, feeling suddenly vulnerable. Their friend Frank was even younger than they were, and now he lay in the hospital recovering from major surgery.

How could she keep this from happening to her own husband? How could she protect her family?

As Bob bowed his head to pray, Charlotte tried to stifle the rising sense that her life was out of control. Once again Bob prayed for his friend Frank, asking God to heal him, and also for strength for Hannah. Charlotte added her own prayer, asking God to help her to trust. To let go.

Bob paused a moment, as if to gather his thoughts, and then asked a blessing on the food. After dinner he was planning to go with Charlotte and Hannah to the hospital to see Frank. It would be the first time Bob had seen his friend since the heart attack and subsequent surgery, and Charlotte was sure the visit was weighing on his mind.

When Bob was done praying, Bill and Pete started talking, as if trying to ease the momentary tension. Food was passed around, and Charlotte helped Madison and Jennifer with their plates, salted their food, and kept them occupied.

"So, Sam, how's work at the airport?" Bill asked, leaning past Anna to catch his nephew's eye.

Sam pushed his salad around with his fork, shrugging. "It's okay, I guess."

"Sam is living through a lack of lucre," Pete said. Then, with a wink toward Anna, who shot him a puzzled frown, he added, "Dana got me a thesaurus."

"How very fortuitous for us," Anna said in a wry tone. "Hopefully now we won't have to hear endless *Princess Bride* quotes." She held up one manicured hand. "And don't even start with that rhyming business."

Pete and Emily exchanged mock horrified looks, and Charlotte had to smile.

"Sam, if you're not making enough money, why don't you go look for another job?" Bill asked, refusing to be waylaid by the silly conversation flowing past him.

"I tried. No one in town is hiring," he said, and then muttered, "except Jenny's Creamery apparently."

Only Charlotte heard that last statement and the sarcasm laced through it, and she wondered again if something was going on between Arielle and Sam.

"What will you do?" Bob asked.

Sam shrugged. "I tried to phone our dad to see if maybe he might have a job for me."

Charlotte's heart skipped a beat. Though she wasn't always privy to the children's conversations with their father, she did like to stay in the loop. Sam had said nothing to her about phoning Kevin.

"Where is Kevin now?" Bill asked, his voice hard. "Last I heard he was working construction."

"Still is," Sam said, sounding a bit defensive. "He's got a job somewhere in Texas."

"I really don't think you should work with your father," Charlotte said gently, hoping her grandson understood her concern and didn't think she was being possessive. "Besides, Texas is far away. I'd like to have you closer to home this last summer before college."

Sam gave Charlotte a lopsided grin. "Don't worry, Grandma. I've got enough to keep me here. I was just kind of desperate."

Charlotte held his steady gaze and felt her shoulders relax. Yes, Kevin Slater was the children's father, and yes, she had no right to stop him from seeing Sam or his other kids. But Kevin hadn't yet created the stable, steady environment he had promised half a year ago, when he crashed into the kids' lives.

That Sam could see this was a blessing indeed. It showed he was more mature than his mother was at his age.

"If you don't mind driving out to River Bend, I might have a job for you," Bill said, helping himself to some more salad. "It's just filing and sorting mail in the office, that kind of thing, but I'll make it worth your while to drive out."

"So what would you consider his while worth?" Pete said.

Bill named a figure, and Sam perked up.

"Really?" he asked.

"I'd need you there a few days a week to start. We can see what happens from there," Bill said.

"That sounds like a good opportunity," Bob said. "You might want to consider it, Sam."

"I might have to quit my job at the airport," Sam returned. "You said I should stick that job out because it doesn't look good on a résumé to jump from job to job."

"But it does look good on a résumé to work at a lawyer's office," Charlotte put in. She knew if Sam wasn't busy over the summer the potential to get into trouble was much greater. If Bill could keep him busy, that would scratch one more worry off her list.

"And if you like it, who knows where it could take you?" Bill said.

"The last thing we need is another lawyer in the family," Pete muttered.

Bill shot him an annoyed look, but Pete just shrugged it off with a grin.

"Think about it, Sam," Bill said, returning his attention to his nephew.

"I don't have to. I'll take it." Sam was smiling now.

"That's excellent. Can you come to my office tomorrow afternoon so we can show you the ropes?"

"I'll have to stop at the airport and put in my resignation before I come. Hopefully Mr. Haffner won't have a problem with me not giving him two weeks' notice." He rocked back in his chair, grinning. "Working in a lawyer's office. Who'd have thunk?"

"Do you think your car can make it to River Bend and back that often?" Charlotte asked.

"Oh, sure," Sam said with all the confidence of adolescence.

When dinner was over, Emily and Dana shooed everyone into the family room, where the men dropped into chairs and Christopher, Madison, and Jennifer pulled out a board game.

Charlotte heard wheels on the gravel in the driveway and knew it was Hannah returning from the hospital. She went to the window and watched as her friend got out of a car and walked up to the front porch.

"Hannah, come in," Charlotte greeted. "How is Frank doing today?"

"He's okay," Hannah said quietly. "But it's difficult to see him lying there with tubes and machines. The nurses are wonderful and are taking good care of him. He's sleeping most of the time still, so it's good for me to try and rest as well, I guess."

"You do look exhausted. Do you want anything to eat before you go lie down?" Charlotte offered.

"I don't want to keep you away from your company." Hannah clasped her hands together.

"It's no trouble," Charlotte assured her.

"You're a good friend."

Charlotte realized again in that moment how lucky she was. She loved being with her family, and she loved watching them interact. Ever since Denise's untimely death, she had held each moment with her family close to her heart, treasuring every second.

Now that Sam was about to start college, she clung to each moment all the more.

Chapter Six

"Do you have to get up this early every morning?" Dana asked Charlotte, stifling a yawn. She wore faded blue jeans and one of Pete's old plaid flannel shirts over a T-shirt. This morning she looked more like a farmer's wife than she had yesterday after church.

It was Monday morning, and the sun hung like a golden ball over the horizon, promising another warm June day.

Today Dana was going to learn how to milk the cow.

"Every morning," Charlotte said, stifling her own yawn.

She'd been at the hospital rather late and then got up early again this morning to begin the usual farm routine. Later this morning she had to take Emily to church to catch the bus leaving for camp, and then there would be another trip to the hospital with Hannah.

She fought down her weariness. Things would come together. They usually did.

"Are you still sure you want to learn how to do this?" Out in the barn, Charlotte led Trudy into the stall and then closed the stanchion around her neck. Dana stood right behind Charlotte, watching every move.

"Of course," Dana said, wiping her palms down the sides of her blue jeans.

"I can get up earlier and milk the cow before I leave for the hospital if you want," Charlotte assured her. "Or I can see if Pete or Bob can take over." Which was a futile suggestion, she knew. Neither Pete nor Bob had the time, busy as they were with fixing the haybine and managing the rest of the farmwork. "It's not easy to milk the cow if you've never done it before."

"I'll have to start sometime," Dana said with a nervous laugh.

Charlotte rinsed out a rag and used it to wash off the cow's udder. When she was done, she set the stool beside Trudy, put the pail in front of the cow's back legs, and then stood aside, indicating that Dana should step closer.

"The first thing you have to do is talk to the cow."

Dana shot her a puzzled look, as if she half expected Charlotte to laugh at her own joke.

"That way she knows exactly where you are," Charlotte explained. "And also, it helps soothe her."

"Okay. Talk to the cow." Dana reached out and petted Trudy on her side. "Hey there. It's me, Dana. You've never met me before, but I'll learn how to get the milk from you."

Charlotte suppressed a quick smile. "That's good. Now just sit down on the stool and put the bucket between your feet." She squatted down beside Dana, so she could demonstrate. "Now to start off, you squeeze the teat between your thumb and forefinger at the very top, pinching it off, so to speak. That keeps the milk from going back up into the udder when you squeeze. Then, one by one, you squeeze with your next finger, then your lazy finger, and your pinkie last, pushing the milk down. And that's all you have to do." A stream of milk sprayed into the metal bucket with a hollow sound.

"While you're squeezing with the one hand, place your other hand on the other teat, pinch it off, and do the same thing. I alternate so I'm squeezing with one and pinching with the other; that creates a nice, easy rhythm." Charlotte showed her.

Dana nodded, and when Charlotte stepped back, she tried it herself. Nothing came out. Charlotte corrected her hold, showed her again, and this time a tiny stream of milk came out.

"Wow! Look at that," Dana exclaimed, clapping her hands. "I'm milking the cow."

Trudy swished her tail and hit Dana on the side of her face. Dana screamed and jumped back, falling off the stool. The noise startled Trudy, who kicked, knocking over the pail.

Charlotte caught Dana and helped her back up, brushing the straw off her shirt.

"Uh, rule number one with large animals," she said, once again holding back her laughter. "Move low and slow. No sudden movements. No sudden noise."

"Well, I broke that rule big time, didn't I?" Dana said, sounding breathless.

"If you want, I can take over."

Dana shook her head. "No. I'll do this. I want to make Pete proud of me."

"I know he already is," Charlotte said, thinking of how

Pete bragged to everyone that "this farmer got himself a teacher for a wife."

"So I'll try again." Dana took a quick breath, as if readying herself for the task, and then righted the pail. She made a face, seeing the pieces of straw clinging to the inside of the pail. "It's dirty," she said.

"No problem." Charlotte reached behind her and picked up a clean pail she had brought along as a precaution. She handed it to Dana, taking the old one away.

Dana looked up at Charlotte with a twinkle in her eyes. "You were kind of suspecting this might happen."

"Happened to me the first time," Charlotte said.

"That makes me feel a lot better," Dana said, turning back to the cow. "Okay, cow, I'm going to do this again, and this time I won't scream like a girl. I promise. You just behave, and I think we'll get along just fine."

She started and got a couple of squirts out, but the next time, nothing. Charlotte corrected her, and Dana did it again. Soon the milk was coming out in steady streams. But Charlotte knew Dana wouldn't last.

Sure enough, a couple of minutes later, she could see Dana was in agony.

"Are your wrists burning yet?" Charlotte asked, trying not to smile.

"Are they ever," Dana panted. "How do you manage?"

"It takes time to build up the muscles," Charlotte said. "When I was first milking the cow, I would start, and Bob would always finish for me. Slowly, I was able to milk the cow longer and longer. I can take over now if you want."

"I feel like a weakling," Dana said, massaging her wrists as she slowly eased away from the cow.

"Your wrists and arms will strengthen in no time," Charlotte assured her as she settled on the stool, leaned her head against the cow's flank, and started milking.

Soon the pail was full, and Dana was full of admiration.

"You did that so quickly. I'll never get done so fast."

"Practice, that's all." Charlotte got up and showed Dana how to let the cow out of the stanchion.

She had time this morning to help Dana, but given her need to be with Hannah, and with Emily headed to camp, Charlotte knew she would have to find another way to help her daughter-in-law learn to be a farmer's wife. Maybe Pete would be willing to take over tomorrow. Frank's doctor was coming in early, and Hannah wanted to be there when he came. Which meant Charlotte had to be there as well.

Dana carried the milk pail back to the house to strain and refrigerate the milk. Charlotte met Christopher scurrying down the driveway, heading toward the toolshed. He looked like he was carrying something in his hands.

"Where are you going, young man? We're having breakfast soon." She shot him a frown. "What happened to your pants?"

Christopher shot her a panicked glance, tucking whatever he was carrying inside his shirt.

"I ripped them . . . and . . . I'm . . . uh . . . just going to check something."

"Okay. I have to take Emily to meet the camp bus later, and then Mrs. Carter and I are going to the hospital. Make sure you put those pants in my patching basket." On top of the other pair of pants she still had to patch . . . in all her spare time.

"Okay," Christopher assured her, his voice trailing behind him as he hurried off.

Charlotte watched him, puzzled as to where he was going. He glanced over his shoulder, faltered, and then veered off toward the horse pasture.

Charlotte was fairly sure that wasn't his initial destination, but it looked like he wasn't going to reveal that to her.

She didn't have time to figure it out and turned back to the house, hurrying up the sidewalk. Dana wanted to make supper tonight, and she had to give her a few pointers on that as well.

She fought down a bit of panic at the thought of all she had to do today. While she appreciated Dana's offer, it was hard to give over control of things she'd been in charge of for so many years.

At least Dana was willing to take them on, Charlotte thought. That was, in fact, a huge help.

"AREN'T YOU READY YET, EMILY?" Charlotte stood in the doorway of her granddaughter's room, shaking her head at the turmoil.

All morning, while Charlotte alternated between writing down things for Dana and talking to Hannah, Emily had been upstairs supposedly packing.

Now, three hours later, her clothing still sat in various piles on the floor, a chair, and the bed.

Emily sat in the middle of the floor holding up a sequined T-shirt. She made a face and then turned the shirt toward Charlotte. "What do you think? Take it or leave it?"

Charlotte tried not to sneak a peak at her watch. She knew it would make Emily feel pressured. But the truth was, the pressure was on. She didn't have time to help Emily make fashion choices.

"I think you should pack whatever is suitable for a Bible camp," Charlotte said, trying to be sensible.

"I don't know what's suitable. I've never been to a camp before, and I've sure never been to a *Bible* camp. Do I pack church clothes? Do I pack just plain clothes? What? I wish Ashley could help."

So did Charlotte.

But she heard the rising panic in Emily's voice. "Okay, I'll see what I can do." Stifling her own frustration, she walked gingerly around the stacks of clothing lying around the room. Goodness, she didn't realize the girl had this many outfits.

"Careful," Emily warned as Charlotte started going through a pile on the floor, "those are the maybes."

"And these?" Charlotte asked, pointing to a much larger pile.

"Possibles."

This would take more work than she had thought.

Fifteen minutes later, they had managed to pack what seemed to be a compromise between Emily's eclectic tastes and what Charlotte thought might be suitable and practical. In spite of trimming down the selections, however, Emily still had to kneel on the suitcase so Charlotte could zip it closed.

Another quick check of the time showed Charlotte they needed to get a move on.

"Now I have to figure out my makeup," Emily said, picking up another empty bag. "Should I take a blow dryer? My flat iron?"

Don't roll your eyes, Charlotte reminded herself, though her much worn patience was reaching transparency.

"You're going to camp. Just pack the minimum," Charlotte said, grabbing Emily's suitcase. "And be downstairs in five minutes."

Chapter Seven

"I hope the bus will wait for us." Grandma gripped the steering wheel the way she did whenever she was uptight.

"I'm sorry we're late." Emily felt bad. "I couldn't find my camera. The one Dad got me."

"If you needed one, you should have asked me," Mrs. Carter said from the front seat. "I have one at my place that I hardly ever use."

Probably an old-school film camera, Emily thought. "Thanks, Mrs. Carter. Christopher was using mine for something, and he wouldn't tell me what." Emily would have gotten mad at him for taking it without asking but figured if she was heading to Bible camp, she should probably be nicer. So she didn't yell at him, and he gave it back to her.

Finally they came around the last corner into the church parking lot. Emily's excitement bubbled up inside when she saw the huge orange bus parked by the curb. Dozens of kids milled about. Suitcases and bags of all colors and sizes lay in a pile on the grass of the church lawn.

This was it. Ten days away from pesky brothers and chores. Ten days of fun, fun, fun. It would have been more fun if she could have taken her cell phone along, but Grandma had said camp was not the place to take a cell phone; so, against her will, Emily had left it in her room.

"Oh, thank goodness. The bus is still there." Grandma pulled into a parking spot and slammed on the brakes, almost sending Mrs. Carter into the dashboard.

"Whoa there, Grandma," Emily said with a nervous laugh, steadying herself on the back of the seat. "We're not that late."

"We would have been if I hadn't hurried," Grandma said, still gripping the steering wheel.

Emily caught Grandma's frown in the rearview mirror. Grandma seemed kind of uptight these days. Emily knew she was worried about Mr. Carter, but she thought the surgery was supposed to make him better.

Grandma rubbed her forehead. Which meant she was getting a headache; Emily immediately felt guilty.

"Grandma, are you sure I should go? Because if you need me at home..." She let the last bit of the sentence fade away, hoping, hoping, hoping Grandma would say no.

Grandma took a breath, as if trying to make up her mind.

Please, please, Emily thought.

Then Grandma looked over her shoulder and smiled. "No, honey. I want you to go. Dana said she would help, and I'm sure she's more than capable."

Emily let her breath go as a wave of relief washed over her. "Okay. Thanks so much, Grandma."

HELPING HANDS | 85

She bolted out of the car, just in case Grandma had second thoughts, dragging her backpack and suitcase out behind her.

"Hey, there you are," Ashley called out from across the lot. She came running toward them, waving a bright pink T-shirt.

"What's that for?" Emily asked as she skidded to a halt in front of her friend.

"I got a bunch of these made up for the girls in our cabin," Ashley said. "You don't have to wear it, but I thought it would be kind of cool."

Emily grinned as she took the shirt and held it up. GIRLS ON THE GO, it said across the front. "You're right. It *is* cool."

Ashley grabbed Emily's suitcase and dragged it down the sidewalk toward the bus. Emily was about to follow when she realized, in the excitement, she hadn't said good-bye.

She walked back to Grandma, dropping her backpack on the ground. "Thanks a ton for letting me go," she said, giving Grandma a quick hug.

"You enjoy yourself, honey," Grandma murmured in her ear, her voice sounding a bit choked. She stroked Emily's head and then pulled back. "I'll miss you."

Emily frowned as she looked into Grandma's eyes. They looked shiny. Was Grandma crying?

"Are you sure you want me to go?" Emily was getting worried.

Grandma waved her off. "Of course. I'm just feeling a little, well, weepy lately." She shrugged and then glanced over at Hannah. "I think it's because of Mr. Carter."

Oh. Of course.

"Hey, Emily." Emily heard a familiar voice and spun around.

Troy stood in front of her, his weight on one leg, his hands in the pockets of his blue jeans, looking at her with a combination of sadness and pleasure. His blond hair hung over his forehead, almost into his green eyes. Then he smiled at her, and Emily's heart did a slow flip. She'd never felt this way about a guy before, and it was exciting and a bit scary at the same time. Was this love? She wished she knew for sure.

"Hey yourself," she said quietly, swinging her backpack back and forth. "I didn't think you'd be here." She'd called his cell phone yesterday to tell him she was going to Bible camp and that she'd be gone for a while, but she'd only gotten his voice mail.

Now, here he was.

"So, you're leaving me for a week and a half?"

Emily nodded as a tiny sliver of unease slid into her mind.

Troy ran a finger down her cheek and gave her a sad smile. "I'm going to miss you. A lot."

"I'm going to miss you too," Emily said.

And suddenly all the excitement of camp melted away with Troy standing in front of her. Could she really leave him for that long just when things seemed to be going so well between them?

She glanced over at Grandma, who was watching them. She had a funny look on her face, like she wasn't sure what to think. Emily knew Grandma and Grandpa weren't too crazy about Troy, but at the same time they didn't know him like she did. He was a really good guy, and he treated her well.

She knew she would miss him, and she also knew Grandma wanted her to stay home anyway. Maybe she shouldn't go to camp. Maybe she should stay home. It would make everyone happier.

Just a few moments ago she couldn't wait to leave and now...

"Hey, Em, you coming?" Ashley called out.

Emily looked from Troy to Ashley and then back to Grandma. "You know, maybe I shouldn't go," she said to Grandma. "I know you need my help."

Grandma frowned as if she wasn't sure. "Oh, honey, you want to go so badly, and Dana has offered to help out."

"Yeah, but..." Emily let the rest of the sentence kind of fade away as she looked back at Troy.

"You can't stay," Ashley wailed. "You have to come. Who'll share my cabin with me? You promised you would come."

"I'll manage just fine," Grandma was saying, giving Emily a quick smile. "You should go. You'll be sorry if you don't."

Emily sighed, wishing she knew what to do. A few moments ago she had been so excited, but now that she saw Troy, she wasn't sure. A couple of days ago Grandma didn't want her to go; now she was encouraging her to leave.

Life could be so confusing sometimes.

"I think you should go too," Troy said, his smile making her heart melt. He stepped just a bit closer, caught her hand, and gave it a squeeze. "Besides, it will make seeing each other again more fun."

"Absence does make the heart grow fonder," Grandma said.

"Please," Ashley begged.

"Okay, okay. I'll go." Emily wasn't sure she had made the right decision, but it did seem like everyone important to her thought she should go.

She gave her grandma another hug. "Bye, Grandma," she said. "I hope things go good for you." Then she turned to Mrs. Carter. "I hope Mr. Carter gets better."

Mrs. Carter nodded, her smile looking a bit forced. "I hope so too, and I hope you have a good time." She caught Emily's hand between her two hands and squeezed. And when she pulled away, Emily discovered Hannah had slipped her two twenty-dollar bills.

Mrs. Carter lifted a finger to her lips. "Don't tell your grandma," she whispered, though Grandma was right there.

Emily knew she should refuse, but at the same time, Mrs. Carter was her grandma's best friend. She didn't have any kids of her own and loved being generous.

"Thank you," she whispered back, tucking the money discreetly into the front pocket of her blue jeans. "I'll spend it wisely."

Then she gave in to an impulse and hugged Mrs. Carter. Tight. Mrs. Carter hesitated a moment and then hugged her back just as hard. "You're a good girl, Emily Slater," she whispered in her ear. "Your grandma and grandpa are lucky to have you."

Emily didn't know what to say, so she just smiled back.

"Well, we'd better go to the hospital," Grandma was saying.

"Why do you have to go there?" Troy asked, frowning just a bit.

"Mr. Carter had major heart surgery on Saturday," Grandma said. "We're going to visit him."

"I'm sorry to hear that," Troy said. "I hope he gets better soon."

Grandma gave Troy a strange look, like she was still trying to figure him out. Then she smiled. "Thank you, Troy. We hope and pray he does too."

Then Grandma and Mrs. Carter walked back to the car. For a moment regret pulled at Emily as she watched Grandma's car pull out of the parking lot.

"I'd better be going too," Troy said, catching her hand between his again. "I've got to get to work. I just wanted to stop by and say good-bye."

"I'm glad you did," Emily said, squeezing his hand back. "Like I said, I'll miss you."

"You'll have a great time."

Emily wasn't so sure now, but another part of her was excited to be away from the farm and off on a new adventure.

Then, to her surprise, Troy bent over and brushed a light kiss over her cheek. "See you in ten days," he said.

Then he left too.

Emily watched as he got into his shiny black pickup; then Ashley was tugging on her arm. "Quit mooning. We've got to get our stuff packed."

A few minutes later Emily was pulled into the milling crowd, almost deafening in its noise and excitement.

Somehow Pastor Jason, their youth leader, managed to get them all organized. Emily helped load their stuff onto the bus as she and Ashley chattered about their plans.

"Okay, everyone. Time to get on the bus," Jason shouted. Emily and Ashley quickly found seats together at the front. Emily recognized some kids from school, but others were unfamiliar to her. Probably kids from surrounding towns.

"A few housekeeping rules before we start," Jason yelled above the noise. The campers slowly settled down; just as Jason was about to continue, a car pulled up in front of the bus and Mrs. Evans got out, waving her arms and yelling.

As another person jumped out of the car, Emily's heart sank.

Nicole Evans.

Would she never get a break from that girl and her sniping? When she hadn't seen Nicole in the parking lot or on the bus, Emily had been so happy.

Guess she had rejoiced just a bit too soon.

Nicole's mother tapped on the door. "My daughter needs to get on the bus," Emily heard her yell. "Open the door."

Emily glanced at Ashley, who was shaking her head with a look of distaste. Looked like she felt the same way.

Jason stepped aside as Nicole climbed the stairs, lugging her suitcase in one hand, her backpack slung over her shoulder, and a pillow tucked under her arm. Her bright orange sweatshirt looked brand-new, as did her distressed blue jeans. In fact, the jeans still had a sticky tape running down the leg proclaiming the size.

Nicole glanced around the bus, looking for a place to sit, and caught Emily's eye. Emily knew it wasn't just her imagination that noticed the slight narrowing of Nicole's eyes, or the way her shoulders lifted, as if she was drawing in a huge sigh.

Emily, figuring she should take the high road, gave her a quick smile and then turned to talk to Ashley. She wasn't letting Nicole spoil her time at camp. She was going to have fun—Nicole or no Nicole.

"SO THIS IS WHERE we keep the files and sort the mail, and you have to make sure you do things in the right order." The woman delivering this rapid-fire information spun around and strode out of the room, her black, curly hair bouncing with every step.

Sam barely had time to look around the file room of his uncle's office before he was on the run again. He couldn't believe a woman wearing a skirt that tight could walk so fast, but Mrs. Pictou was greased lightning in bright red high heels.

When Sam had arrived at the office that afternoon Uncle Bill was standing in the reception area, flipping through some papers. He hardly recognized his uncle in his dark blue suit, blinding white shirt, and red-and-blue-striped tie. He really looked like a lawyer now. Sam felt just a bit intimidated.

But Uncle Bill chatted with him, welcoming him to the firm. Then he handed Sam over to Mrs. Jocelyn Pictou, explaining that she was a paralegal who assisted his uncle and his partner, Mr. Donald Simpson. Sam had no idea what a paralegal was, but whatever it was, Mrs. Pictou was quick.

Sam jogged to keep up with her, clutching the tie Grandma insisted he wear. Ditto the white shirt because none of Sam's other shirts, mostly T-shirts, work shirts, and hoodies, passed muster as suitable for wearing in a law office, according to Grandma.

"And of course this is Mr. Stevenson's office," Mrs. Pictou called out, waving one manicured hand to her right. Sam chanced a look through the large open door. Uncle Bill was leaning against his desk, his hands crossed over his chest, laughing at a joke with the person sitting in the chair in front of him.

Uncle Bill looked up as Sam passed and gave him a curt nod. That was it. Like he didn't even know who Sam was.

"Hello, Sam." Lena, Uncle Bill's secretary, looked up at him from the computer she was working on. She looked a bit younger than Grandma, and her brown hair didn't have as many gray streaks in it. She seemed nice, at least compared with Mrs. Pictou. "Good to have you here. I hope you enjoy the work."

"I do too," Sam said.

"If you have any questions, you can ask me. Might not be able to answer them all, but I'll give it my best shot." She gave him another quick smile and then reached over to answer the phone.

"Are you coming, Sam?" Mrs. Pictou barked.

Sam resisted the urge to salute. Uncle Pete had warned him not to get cocky while he worked here. Sam certainly didn't intend to mess up; the money was too good.

Half an hour later his head was still spinning from all the information. Working in this office was very different from working at the airport, with its mess and smell and noise and dirt.

Here everything was neat, clean, and tidy, and the only smell was the coffee brewing in the break room. For a panicky moment he wondered if he would fit in at all. Then he pushed that thought aside. He had to. Now that he had officially quit at the airport and there was no other job in Bedford to be had, he didn't have any backup.

"Coffee?" Mrs. Pictou asked, holding up a mug. He shook his head and got a cup of water from the water cooler instead. "Another job you'll be in charge of is making sure this coffeepot is always full. Lawyers live off caffeine and billable hours," she continued. "The hours you can't do much about, but the caffeine you can. So just make sure the pot is filled all the time so Mr. Stevenson and Mr. Simpson—and I, of course—always have coffee when we need it."

Sam had rarely made coffee and was a little bummed to think this might be part of his job. *Suck it up, Slater*, he reminded himself, thinking again of the pay Uncle Bill had promised him.

The rest of the day passed in a blur of sorting mail, making coffee, delivering mail, making coffee, learning how the filing system worked, figuring out how to operate the copy machine and change the toner, and learning who to call when things weren't working. He learned how to see which case belonged to Uncle Bill and which case belonged to Mr. Simpson, which papers were important and which ones could be set aside.

And he was getting really good at making coffee and cleaning up the break room.

If Emily could see me now, he thought as he dried off another mug. *She'd have a good laugh.*

"Sam, there are some files sitting on the in-tray in the file room," Mrs. Pictou called out from the doorway of the break room.

Startled, Sam just about dropped the mug. "I'm sorry," he said, putting everything down. "I forgot about them."

"We work with very, very important information here," she snapped. "This isn't the mindless work you've done in the past."

Sam tried not to get ticked at her. The work he'd done before had been important too. If he didn't put enough fuel in the planes they'd fall out of the sky.

"Those files better get put away. Immediately."

He kept his thoughts to himself and jogged over to the file room to put the files away. Immediately.

Though he had worked physically harder at the airport and on the farm than he did in the law office, by late afternoon Sam felt more exhausted than he had in months. This job wasn't going to be the walk in the park he'd thought it would be.

It was already five forty-five. Technically the office was

closed, and he was supposed to have been done by five. He closed the door of the file room and headed out.

He paused at the doorway to Uncle Bill's office. His uncle sat at his desk, his tie loosened, his head resting on his hand as he paged through a file in front of him. A basket of files sat on one corner of his desk beside his computer, and three more lay on the floor; books were open everywhere.

Uncle Bill looked up when he saw Sam. He grinned and leaned back. "How was your first day?"

"Tiring." Sam didn't know if he was allowed to walk into the office, so he stayed in the doorway. "I never knew there could be so much paper in one office."

Uncle Bill laughed, stretching his arms over his head. "Yeah. We love to keep the paper companies going, even though computers were supposed to change all that." He lowered his arms and then glanced back at the file in front of him; Sam guessed he wanted to get back to work.

"Say hi to Aunt Anna and the girls for me," Sam said.

Uncle Bill just nodded.

Sam trudged through the hallway and down the stairs.

A few minutes later he was in his car and heading home. Just before the turnoff to Bedford he slowed, wondering if he had time to stop in at Jenny's Creamery before he went home.

Yesterday after church, he'd managed to talk to Arielle for a little while, but she had had to go to a family dinner in Harding. Tonight she was working at Jenny's—tomorrow night and Wednesday night too.

So if he didn't stop, he wouldn't see Arielle at all today. He made a sudden decision, turned off the highway, and drove into town. Maybe he'd grab an ice cream at the creamery.

He parked his car. Though the setting sun helped cool things off, it was still warm out, and the creamery looked busy. He stepped inside and saw Arielle handing an older couple their ice creams. Her face was flushed, and strands of hair had come loose from her ponytail.

"Hey, that's our order." A plump man in his late twenties barked at Arielle. He wore a denim jacket over a stained T-shirt, and Sam could see a snake tattoo crawling up his neck.

Arielle looked at the cones and then at the couple across the counter. "I'm so sorry," she said. She took the cones back, rewrapped them, and handed them to the other customer.

"That took you long enough," the tattooed man said, reaching for the cones. "The service in this place is lousy."

"I'm so sorry. Things are a little hectic," Arielle explained.

Sam leaned against the wall, waiting for a moment when he could talk to Arielle.

"You still got it wrong. I'm the one with the chocolate, my girlfriend is the one with the pistachio, and we need two more cones. Get it right."

Sam's eyes narrowed as the customer continued to snap at Arielle.

"I said I was sorry." Arielle sounded close to tears. "Just give me the cones and I'll do them again."

"What were you doing? Dreaming about your boyfriend?" the man said, grinning at his three friends, as if trying to get them to share the joke.

Sam had had enough. He straightened up and walked over to the counter. The guy doing the complaining had about twenty pounds on him, but Sam was taller.

"I don't think you need to talk to her like that," Sam said, trying to keep his voice quiet.

"Sam, what are you doing here?" Arielle pressed her hand against her chest, frowning at him. Her reaction wasn't encouraging.

"So is this the boyfriend you were daydreaming about?" The tattooed man's grin made Sam even angrier.

"Just leave her alone. She just started working here," he said.

"Sam. Please." Arielle frowned at him. "It doesn't matter."

"Good idea, missy," the man was saying. "Wouldn't want to mess up that pretty face of his."

Sam was really angry now, but Arielle had come around the counter and was pulling him away. People were starting to look at them, and Sam wasn't sure what to do. He was a guy, and guys were supposed to defend their girlfriends against creeps like this character.

"Please, please, don't make a scene." Arielle gave one final tug, yanking him behind the counter toward the coolers. She pulled him around the corner. "What are you doing here?" she hissed.

"I came for some ice cream and to see you."

"Why did you talk back to that customer?" she asked.

Sam just stared at her as she stood in front of him, her

clenched hands planted on her hips, her blue eyes snapping at him in anger.

He held up his hands. "Hey, I'm not the one who was insulting you." What was wrong with her? He thought he was helping her out.

"No. But you're the one who may make me lose my job."

Sam laughed at the thought. "Jenny wouldn't fire you."

Arielle bit her lip as she seemed to calm down. "Maybe not, but I want to do a good job here. I need a good résumé for when I go to college. I don't want any problems with customers."

"Hey, you've got stellar recommendations coming out your ears." Sam was puzzled at the change in his girlfriend. She seemed super stressed. "What's wrong, Arielle? Why are you so prickly tonight?"

Arielle bit her lip and looked away. "It's just...this is a lot of work, and I'm thinking about school coming up and paying for books and stuff." She blew out a sigh. "Just lots of things on my mind, that's all."

"Hey. You don't have to worry about all that." Sam reached out and touched his finger to her cheek. "You're a fantastic student, and I'm sure Jenny thinks you're a great worker."

"Maybe you're right," Arielle said.

"Of course I'm right. You've got nothing to worry about." He stroked her cheek just to make his point. "And you've got me," he said, hoping his small joke would make her smile.

She looked up at him, her expression serious. Then her lips shifted, forming a hesitant smile. "Yeah. I've got you."

"Still waiting out here," the customer called out.

"Sorry, Sam. I gotta go." Arielle stood up on her tiptoes, brushed a quick kiss over his cheek, and then left.

Sam watched her go, wondering what had just happened. Everything between them was weird. And that kiss. Like something she'd give a puppy.

He shrugged the feeling off. Arielle was always a serious person; that was all. She just had a lot on her mind.

But now he had to leave through the back way. No way was he going through the front so that tattooed loser could laugh at him and bug him about getting his girlfriend to rescue him.

He trudged back to his car, his feet sore from standing on them all day. As he turned onto the highway, he realized he hadn't had a chance to tell Arielle about his own new job.

He wondered if she'd even care.

Chapter Eight

"Here we are. Camp Whispering Pines," Pastor Jason called out from the front of the bus as it rocked to a halt. He stood up with his hands on his hips, his goofy cap askew on his head. "Thank you for riding with our company, Wheels on the Road. Our motto: We keep most of our wheels on the road." His joke was greeted with a few polite chuckles and a lot of impolite groans.

Emily thought it was funny.

"Before disembarking please ensure all luggage is claimed; all cell phones must be deposited in the bin beside me. If you are found with a cell phone on your person at any time during camp you will be fined, flogged, and thrown into the lake." He shot a mock scowl at everyone. "I'm not kidding about the flogging."

Guess Grandma was right about the cell phones after all, Emily thought.

"Cabins are assigned," Jason was saying, "so there's no need to mutilate and harm one another in the process of getting to your new homes. I'll be giving out your cabin numbers as you disembark. If you have any questions, ask me."

He held up a bright yellow T-shirt. "All camp counselors and leaders will be wearing one of these so you know who you can pester about when the concession stand is open and how you really don't want to get stuck doing dishes . . . again. So have a good time and remember who you are."

With that the bus doors opened, and twenty-four kids tried to get out of the bus all at once.

When Emily got out, she looked around, eager to check out this camp Ashley was so excited about. The bus had parked in a main square. A flag fluttered from a flagpole in the center of the square. A huge barn-looking building with unfinished wood stood to one side. It had huge double doors and a cross on the roof. Beside that was a long, low building made of cement blocks with a tin roof. Over the double doors a sign said DINING HALL.

Through the tall trees she caught a glimpse of the lake and all around them, small cabins lay scattered in the trees.

This was the camp Ashley was raving about? It looked like someone had slapped it together in one summer.

"Awesome!" Ashley exclaimed, looking at a piece of paper Jason had given her. "Let's go, Emily."

Emily gave the camp another quick look and then grabbed her backpack, claimed her suitcase, and followed her friend down a winding path through the trees.

"We scored the best cabin," Ashley said as she pushed

open the door of a small, wooden building. "We totally lucked out getting this one."

Disappointment filtered through Emily as she dropped her suitcase on the wooden floor. This place looked like the rest of the camp.

When Ashley talked about the cabins they were staying in, she had imagined cute log lodges with couches and chairs and bedrooms and a fireplace. Not this rough-hewn building with sets of bunk beds and a bathroom with a tin shower and flimsy curtain. A bathroom that didn't have shelves big enough for her stuff, let alone all the other girls'.

The sun barely shone through a couple of windows, one in each peak of the roof; two bare lightbulbs hung from the ceiling, and that was it. Ashley said it was so people couldn't see inside.

And there was only one electrical outlet for eight girls? What was up with that?

"If this is the best one, I'd hate to see the worst one," Emily said with a quick laugh as she put away the last of her clothes in the metal locker that was supposed to be her closet.

"I know, I know. It's a bit rough, but that's part of the charm." Ashley jumped on her bed, almost hitting her head on the ceiling. "Get your stuff put away. We have to make sure we get to orientation in time."

Ashley jumped off the bed and was about to put her own stuff away when a girl called her from the doorway. With a squeal, Ashley ran outside and soon was chattering a mile a minute with, Emily guessed, an old friend from previous camps.

Emily rearranged some of her clothes and listened at the same time, wondering if she would make friends like that as well.

Ashley wasn't gone long; she returned just as Emily was about to head for the bathroom with her cosmetics bag.

"Whoa, Nelly. Where are you going with that?" she asked.

"I'm thinking the bathroom?"

"No, no, no. You never, ever put your own cosmetics in the shared bathroom. Recipe for running out of lotion, conditioner, and mascara." Ashley grabbed Emily by the arm and tugged her back to her locker. "This is where you stash your stuff." Ashley's mouth fell open as she opened Emily's locker. "If you can find room. Why did you bring so much stuff?"

"I didn't know what to bring. Grandma was after me to make sure I packed enough warm clothes and enough summer clothes, and I didn't know if I had to dress up for church..." Emily sighed, already feeling dumb. Thank goodness none of the other girls were here. A couple of them had arrived before Emily and Ashley and had already claimed their bunks, but they had left again.

"Don't worry. You can move some of your stuff to my locker; otherwise you'll get razzed about being a beauty queen."

"Beauty queen?"

Ashley shrugged. "That's what we call the girls who change outfits all the time."

"I wish you would have told me some of this stuff sooner," Emily said. "I don't want to get hassled."

"Move some of this stuff, and we're all good." Ashley made a quick switch. "And now you've got room for your cosmetics and stuff. Oooh. Did you bring your flat iron?"

"For sure. And nail polish."

Ashley grinned. "All the colors?"

"Most of them."

"Awesome. We can do pedicures. That will make you a big hit."

Emily felt increasingly confused. Pedicures were okay, but changing clothes too often wasn't?

Ashley must have sensed her confusion and patted her on the shoulder. "You'll catch on quick enough. I've been to camp enough times. Just do what I do."

Some girls were laughing just outside the cabin; the laughter got louder and suddenly the door of the cabin flew open, letting in the bright summer sun. Emily's eyes had grown accustomed to the half-light in the cabin, and she had to blink.

At first she couldn't see who was in the doorway, just their silhouettes.

The girls paused. They weren't laughing anymore, and Emily wondered what was going on.

"Oh, this is just great. I can't believe we got assigned to a cabin with *you* girls."

Emily's heart fell into her sneakers. Nicole Evans.

Emily and Ashley had a chance to exchange horrified looks, and then Nicole walked toward them.

"Hey, Nicole," Emily said by way of greeting. "The two sets of bunks by the door are still available. The other ones are taken."

Nicole stepped into the cabin, her eyes flicking over the bunks. "I notice you've got the best beds," was all she said. "If I were you, I would have taken the ones by the door."

"So what are you complaining about?" Emily said. "You got them."

Ashley snorted, trying to hold her laughter in. Then she recovered. "You know how it goes, Nicole. It's always first come, first serve," Ashley said with a quick grin. "But it doesn't matter where we sleep because at camp we don't sleep."

"Speak for yourself," Nicole said, tossing her suitcase on the bottom bunk by the door.

"Who's your friend?" Ashley asked as another girl followed Nicole into the cabin.

"This is Ellen," Nicole said. "My friend from last year."

"Hey, Ellen, good to meet you," Ashley said. "I'm Ashley. This is Emily."

Emily gave her a quick smile just as Nicole glanced over at Emily and frowned. "What are you staring at?"

Be nice. Be nice, Emily told herself.

But she couldn't hold it in any longer. "I'm staring at the label still stuck to your pants." Emily angled her head to one side as if to read it as Nicole looked down as well. "I didn't know you were a size—"

"Never mind," Nicole blurted as she ripped the size strip off the pants.

Emily just smiled, shoved her hands into the pockets of her blue jeans, and followed Ashley out of the cabin. When they were out of earshot, she blew out a sigh. "Why, of all people, did we have to end up with *her* in our cabin?"

"Maybe God is trying to teach us patience," Ashley said.

Emily shot her a frown, but her friend was serious. "I wish He'd use someone different to teach us."

Ashley slung her hand over Emily's shoulder. "It will be okay. There'll be other girls in the cabin who don't know Nicole or us. The dynamics are always different at camp."

"I sure hope so."

"Now let's go check out the beach."

A light breeze whipped up a few waves on the lake as they got closer. A group of canoes were stacked upside down on some kind of rack by the boathouse.

A long wooden dock extended into the water and then made a T. A tall boy sat cross-legged on one end of the T, facing away from them. He wore only a T-shirt and blue jeans and didn't seem to mind the cool wind coming off the lake, tossing around his longish dark hair.

"Who is that?" Emily asked, zipping up her hoodie and shoving her hands into the pockets. He looked to be about as old as Sam, so he probably wasn't a counselor.

Ashley looked in the direction Emily was indicating and then shrugged. "No one I've seen before. This must be his first time here."

"He looks kind of lonely."

Ashley nudged Emily. "He also looks kind of hot."

"Hey," Emily protested. "I have a boyfriend."

Ashley laughed. "You wouldn't be the first girl to forget about a guy at home when she comes to camp."

"I'm not like that."

They walked along the beach toward the dock, the sand hard under their feet. The young man stood and stretched. He looked out over the lake for a bit longer and then turned and walked toward them, his hands in the back pockets of his pants and his head down. He had a kind of loose-limbed walk. Not quite a saunter, but not slouching. Like he had things on his mind.

He stepped off the dock just as Ashley and Emily came near. He stopped, as if startled when he saw them.

"Hey," he said quietly, glancing from Ashley to Emily.

"Hey, yourself," Emily said. "You just hanging out?"

He nodded. "My name is Mike."

"Emily." She pointed her thumb over her shoulder. "This is Ashley. My friend."

Mike nodded at Ashley and then, curiously, turned back to Emily. "So I'm guessing you're also a camper?"

"Yeah. First time. Ashley asked me to come, and I thought I would give it a try. It's fun so far. Well, we just got here, but I think it will be fun." Why was she babbling so much? Usually it was Ashley who was the yappy one.

"That's great. I hope you enjoy it." He gave her a quick smile, and then their eyes met and held.

Just for a moment Emily saw a pain in his eyes that was so familiar to her, it almost hurt. He didn't look away either, as if he felt it too.

Emily was the first one to break the connection as a self-conscious flush crept up her neck.

"Well, see you around," he said, taking a step away.

As he walked away, Emily couldn't keep from turning around to watch him go. Just as he got to the grass, he turned and looked back.

Directly at her.

Chapter Nine

This thing was way too heavy.

Christopher gave the wooden handle of the plow another tug and then sat down in the grass. Toby dropped down beside him, and Christopher absently patted her head.

"There's no way I can pull that out by myself," he grumbled to Toby, wiping some sweat from his forehead. It was Tuesday morning. Sam was off at work. Emily was gone, and Grandma and Mrs. Carter had gone to the hospital. He felt all alone.

Toby turned her head toward him, her eyes looking sad.

Christopher had been struggling all morning trying to get this old horse-drawn plow free from the grass. Maybe he should just give up. There was no way he could carry out his plan by himself.

He wished Uncle Pete could help him. Or Grandpa.

He walked around to the front of the tractor shed and then went inside. The farm truck was parked inside, and Christopher could hear the radio playing from one corner of the shop.

Uncle Pete and Grandpa stood by the workbench, pounding on something. At least Uncle Pete was pounding; Grandpa was telling him where to pound.

"Be careful, Pete. We can't afford to wreck this thing."

"I'm being careful. Just trust me."

Uncle Pete's voice got hard, like it did when he was angry, and Christopher was just about to leave. He had found out the hard way it was best to just stay clear when Uncle Pete and Grandpa weren't getting along. People who were fighting made his stomach hurt.

Then Grandpa looked over and saw him. "Hey, son. What's up?"

Christopher walked closer. "Are you really busy?" he asked.

"Yeah. Kind of. We're working on the irrigation pump," Grandpa said. The frown on his face didn't look encouraging. "Why?"

"Well I was by the old shed in back? And I saw some stuff? And, well, I thought . . ."

"I thought I told you to stay out of there," Grandpa said, the frown lines on his forehead getting even deeper.

"I'm careful," Christopher said. "And I found some neat stuff. And I was wondering . . ."

"We should really pull that shed down," Uncle Pete said. But he was talking to Grandpa.

"One of these days. For now we need to get this pump going."

"And the haybine fixed."

Christopher shifted back and forth a bit, hoping they would remember him, but they were too busy. So he went back outside and dropped onto the grass. It was still wet from dew, but he didn't care. He didn't care about anything.

It was going to be a long, long summer.

"Hey, Christopher. What are you doing?"

Christopher jumped as his aunt Dana sat down in the grass beside him.

"Nothin'," Christopher said.

"I see. What were you doing before I came?"

Christopher wrapped his arms around his knees and rested his chin on top. "I was trying to get Uncle Pete or Grandpa to help me pull out that old plow." Christopher just pointed at the long wooden handle sticking out from the grass.

"That's pretty heavy. Can't Uncle Pete or Grandpa help you?"

"They're busy." Christopher heard the clang of a wrench dropping on the cement floor of the tractor shed "I found a whole bunch of other stuff too. I thought it would be kind of fun . . ." He stopped there. Aunt Dana was busy too. She probably didn't have time to hear what he wanted to do.

Or to help him.

"Fun to do what?" Aunt Dana asked.

Christopher pulled in a deep breath and then sighed. "Fun to maybe make a float or something for the Fourth of July parade."

"Wow. That would be a lot of work."

Christopher thought the same. "That's why it's just an idea."

"Well, I think it's a great idea. I'll tell you what, though. Why don't you show me what you found? Then you can help me with the chickens, and maybe I can help you with your float idea." Dana got up and brushed the grass off her pants.

"What do you have to do with the chickens?" Christopher asked as he stood.

"Get the eggs. I helped your grandma milk the cow this morning and before she left, she asked me to gather the eggs and make sure the waterer works for the cows. I'm not exactly sure how to get the eggs."

"They're in the nesting boxes," Christopher said, surprised Aunt Dana didn't know that.

"But, well, you see, there are chickens in the boxes. They give me the willies."

Christopher had to laugh. "Emily was afraid of them too when we first came here. You just have to put your hand under them and don't get nervous if they peck."

"Right. But I do get worried, so I thought you could help me if I help you." Aunt Dana tilted her head to one side and gave him a big smile, and Christopher had to laugh. "So let's look at what you found, and then you can help me with my chores."

She was serious.

Christopher jumped to his feet and walked quickly through the long grass again, leading Aunt Dana toward the old shed behind the tractor shed. "There's some stuff in here and an old truck behind the little building, in the trees," he said as he worked his way to the rear of the shed, growing more excited about his plan. "Uncle Pete and Grandpa would never let me go in here because they said it was dangerous, but I think it's okay."

He slipped inside the building. Then he turned to look behind him. Aunt Dana was a bit taller, but she got inside okay.

"Okay, I can see why your Grandpa wasn't crazy about

you coming in here," Aunt Dana said. "The rest of this roof looks like it could fall in any minute."

"That beam is holding it up, so it will be okay," Christopher said, pointing it out to her. "This is some of the stuff I've found, and I don't know what it is." He had piled some of the things together in what looked like a safer corner of the shed.

Aunt Dana looked it all over; then she bent over and picked up the two sticks attached with a piece of leather. "I'm not sure, but I kind of think this is a flail."

"Flail? How does it work?" Christopher asked.

"From what I remember, the farmers used to cut down the wheat with a scythe; then they left it to dry, and finally they laid it out and beat it with a flail. That separated the kernels from the chaff."

"How do you know all that stuff?" Christopher asked.

"I learned it in a history class in college. I never had a chance to use it because I ended up teaching English instead of history." Aunt Dana put aside the sticks and looked over some of the other stuff. "Wow, you did find all kinds of treasures."

"I took some pictures and thought I might find the stuff on the Internet and learn what it is," Christopher said.

"Or we could ask your grandpa."

"He said he was busy."

"Well, I'm sure he can't be busy all the time. Didn't he and Pete already finish the planting?" Aunt Dana asked.

Christopher shook his head. Aunt Dana didn't understand. On the farm there was always, always something else to do.

"Why don't you help me get the eggs, and then we can ask him to come and have a look?" Aunt Dana asked.

"Okay. We can try." Christopher wasn't as sure as Aunt Dana was that Grandpa would want to help, but if *she* asked, maybe he would.

They walked together to the chicken house, and Christopher slowly pushed the door open.

"Low and slow," he heard Aunt Dana say. "Low and slow."

Some of the chickens were in the coop, walking around, pecking the ground, looking for some leftover food. About half of the nest boxes had chickens in them.

"How about I get the eggs out of the boxes that don't have chickens in them," Aunt Dana proposed, walking over to the boxes and picking up some of the eggs.

"Did you bring a pail?" Christopher asked, carefully sliding his hand under one chicken. The hen made a gurgling kind of sound, like it was warning him, but Christopher didn't pay any attention. He felt three nice, warm eggs under the chicken and gently pulled them out, one at a time.

Aunt Dana put the eggs in the pocket of her coat and shook her head. "I didn't think there'd be that many."

Christopher pulled his tucked-in shirt out of his pants and made a cradle for the eggs. Then he went to the next chicken. When he was done he walked over to Aunt Dana, who was checking to make sure the chickens had enough water.

"You can put the eggs in my shirt," he said.

"That's okay. You look like you've already got more than enough there."

They walked back to the house; just before they got

there, Uncle Pete yelled to them from across the yard. "Hey, you two. Where you going?"

Aunt Dana spun around, grinning. She ran over to Uncle Pete and gave him a big hug. Then she pulled back, and Christopher saw a funny look come over her face. He knew exactly what had happened.

She had forgotten about the eggs.

"What's this?" Uncle Pete rubbed his hand over something wet on his coveralls.

"I think it's egg," Aunt Dana said, pulling her coat away from herself. "I think I got it all over me. How could I be so silly?"

Uncle Pete burst out laughing. "Happens to everyone. I hate to count the times I've made a quick run through the chicken coop, picked up a couple of eggs, and forgotten all about them. Until I sat on them or squished them." He patted Aunt Dana on the shoulder. "All part of the learning process."

"Some kind of farmer's wife I am. I feel so silly."

"Don't worry. You don't look silly," Uncle Pete said as he helped Aunt Dana take her coat off. "Let's see what we can salvage here." He pulled open one pocket, looked inside, and then peeked inside the other one; he shook his head. "That was quite a hug," he said, making a face. "Total, mass destruction."

He whistled for Toby and then walked over to her food bowl and dumped as much of the egg mess as he could into the dish.

"Make sure you take the egg shells out," Christopher reminded him. He didn't want Toby to get sick.

"I guess we won't be having eggs for supper," Aunt Dana said.

Pete frowned. "Mom won't be back by then?"

"No. She asked me to feed you guys." Aunt Dana took her soggy coat from Uncle Pete, holding it away from her. "So, instead of eggs, what should we have?"

"Any kind of food I don't make myself is good," Uncle Pete said. "We'll be in at six thirty. But I gotta run. Christopher, did you check on the horses this morning?"

"But that's Emily's . . ." Christopher sighed and shook his head as he realized Emily was gone. Of course. She was having fun at camp and getting away from chores while he was here at home doing her work.

And Sam was helping Uncle Bill; he was probably having fun too. Christopher sighed; he always got the short end of the stick.

"Why don't we check the horses together, and then we can go look up some stuff on the computer," Aunt Dana said as Uncle Pete left.

Christopher sighed but figured at least he had someone willing to help him, so he should accept her offer.

"So tell me, what were you thinking of in terms of a float?" Aunt Dana asked him as they walked toward the pasture fence. "What would you put it on, and how would you pull it?"

"I was hoping we could use the old farm truck to pull the hay wagon. We'd have to put fringy stuff on the edge of the wagon so it looks like it's floating."

"We'd need a theme," Aunt Dana said. She snapped her fingers. "Something historical so we could use the antiques in the shed."

She sounded really excited.

"Like pioneers, you mean?" Christopher asked.

"Exactly like that." Aunt Dana was walking faster now. "We'll check the horses like you're supposed to do, and then we'll go back to the house and work on some ideas for the float while I make lunch; maybe we'll have time to find those old things on the computer too."

They got to the corral and Dana walked inside. "So what are we supposed to check for?" she asked, looking back at Christopher.

"Mostly just make sure they're not hurt. Or make sure they don't have any porcupine quills stuck in their noses."

"What do we do if we find that?"

"Then we have to get Uncle Pete or Grandpa." Christopher looked at Dana, a bit surprised she didn't know stuff like that.

The horses were way out in the pasture; Christopher groaned.

"What's the matter?" Aunt Dana asked. She sounded a bit worried.

"Nothing. Really. We just have to go all the way out there so we can take a good look at them." For just a minute he was tempted to leave them be, but he knew Uncle Pete would ask and Aunt Dana would know he hadn't checked them properly.

So he started the long walk out there. Britney was the first to look up when they came closer.

Britney started walking toward them, her almost-two-year-old offspring, Stormy, right behind her. As the pair left the small herd, the other horses looked up and then started following Britney, as if afraid they might miss out on something. Christopher watched them as they came closer. They looked fine. Ben had been limping, but he seemed OK now.

"Anything else we're supposed to look for?" Aunt Dana asked.

"Nope." He looked them over again. "I don't see any porcupine quills, and their legs are okay, and they don't have any cuts. Princess is usually the one who gets into trouble, but she looks good too."

"Okay then. While we're out here, let's go work with your lamb, and then we can go to the house."

Christopher spun around, excited to get to work on the float. He had a bunch of ideas, but he was sure Aunt Dana had even more.

His lamb was lying down when they got to him, so Christopher got the halter from the barn. It took awhile to catch him, but soon he was leading Magic around the pen.

"You've really got that lamb trained well," Aunt Dana said, sounding quite impressed.

"He's been pretty easy to work with now that he's learned not to get out all the time," Christopher agreed. He gave the halter a tug, and Magic followed along nicely behind him until it was time to get him to stop. Then Magic kept going, pulling Christopher's arm away. He tugged and tugged and almost fell over.

"Obviously needs a bit of work yet," Aunt Dana said with a chuckle. "When do you have to have Magic trained by?"

"For the fair."

Aunt Dana was about to say something else when Christopher thought he heard Uncle Pete yelling. What was going on?

He quickly pulled the halter off Magic and ran to the

fence. He climbed up, still holding the halter, in time to see Britney, Stormy, Princess, Ben, Shania, and Tom racing down the driveway and heading toward the road, hooves pounding and dust flying up behind them.

What had happened?

Uncle Pete was behind them, but Christopher knew there was no way he could catch them. Uncle Pete stopped in the middle of the driveway, yanked off his hat, and threw it on the ground.

He looked over and saw Christopher and Aunt Dana hanging over the fence. "How did those horses get out?" Uncle Pete yelled at Christopher, his voice hard and tight.

"I don't know," Christopher said, swallowing down a bit of panic. "They were way out in the pasture when we checked on them."

Uncle Pete snatched his hat off the ground and shoved it back on his head. "We have to go after them now. That'll take forever." He blew out his breath, glanced sideways, and then shook his head. "No wonder they got out. You left the gate open, Christopher. How many times do I have to remind you to close the gate? I don't have time for this baloney," he said, his voice getting louder and louder.

Christopher wished Uncle Pete wouldn't be so angry. It wasn't his fault.

"I was the one who left the gate open," Aunt Dana said, her voice quiet.

Uncle Pete spun around, and for a moment Christopher thought he would yell at her too. Then he pressed his lips together, like he was holding his words back, and Christopher felt really bad.

"You should have double-checked, Christopher,"

Uncle Pete said. He grimaced and then motioned for Christopher to follow him. "I'll get some halters; you get a pail of oats. Meet me at the truck right away. Hurry."

"What can I do?" Aunt Dana asked.

"Close the gate for now. But as soon as you hear us coming, I want you to make sure the gate is open so the horses can run in."

Aunt Dana just nodded, but Christopher could see she wasn't very happy.

Neither was Uncle Pete, and it was all his fault.

Christopher ran to the barn as fast as he could, grabbed a pail, and scooped some oats into it. Then he ran back to the truck just as Uncle Pete got in.

"You know you have to close gates behind you," Uncle Pete said as he slapped at the gearshift. Now he sounded really mad. "Aunt Dana isn't used to being on a farm. She doesn't know about that kind of stuff."

Christopher wanted to say something to stand up for himself, but he could see Uncle Pete wouldn't listen, so he didn't say anything.

As they drove, they looked back and forth, hoping they would find the horses. For a while, all they saw was hoofprints on the road. Dumb horses. Why did they want to run away from home?

"There they are." Uncle Pete slammed on the brakes, and Christopher glanced in the direction he was pointing.

They were halfway across a newly planted field.

"Great. Now we're going to get into trouble with the neighbor." Uncle Pete sighed as he parked the truck.

"What should I do?" Christopher kept his voice quiet, hoping Uncle Pete wouldn't be so angry.

"Just get the oats. Then follow me and hope the horses don't decide to run away again."

Christopher jumped out of the cab and clambered into the back of the truck. He handed Uncle Pete the halters and moved the pail of oats to the back so he could reach it better.

"I just don't have time for this," Uncle Pete muttered as he picked up the pail, which made Christopher feel even worse.

The horses saw them coming; Tom lifted up his head and his tail and started trotting away. Christopher could feel his heart pounding in his chest. This wouldn't work. He just had a feeling.

The other horses looked up, and then Stormy kicked up her heels, bucked once, and ran after Tom.

This wasn't going well at all. Uncle Pete growled, and they ran back to the truck and jumped in. They raced the truck down the road, trying to get ahead of the horses. The horses stopped, and they got out of the cab and tried again. And again the horses took off.

Half an hour and four fields later, the horses finally stood still long enough for Uncle Pete to coax them with some oats. Britney was the first one to come back. She was always hungry. When Uncle Pete got a halter on her, he handed it to Christopher, glaring at him. "Hang on to this," he said, sounding very growly. "Don't even think about letting go."

Christopher grabbed the lead rope and hung onto it as tight as he could. If Britney took off, she would have to drag him along. He just hoped she wouldn't get any funny ideas. She was a lot bigger than he was.

Britney whinnied, looking around for Stormy, and Christopher's heart jumped a bit; but then Stormy came closer, and Britney settled down.

Uncle Pete walked up to Stormy and slipped a halter over her head as well. Soon the other horses came ambling up and Uncle Pete had them haltered and ready to go back home.

"We'll have to walk them back to the farm," Uncle Pete said, sounding grim. "Dad and I will come back for the truck."

Christopher groaned. He figured they were at least five miles from the house. By the time they walked all that way, it would be time for Dana to start making supper. Then she and Uncle Pete would go home.

And she wouldn't have time to help him with the float.

If he had just skipped checking the horses, none of this would have happened.

Chapter Ten

"When did the doctor say you could come home?" Bob leaned forward in the plastic chair they had hauled into Frank's hospital room, his hands jostling and his knees nervously jogging.

Charlotte pressed back her smile at the sight. Bob hated coming to the hospital. Reminded him of his own vulnerability, she thought.

"They figure by the end of the week. Friday, maybe Saturday," Frank said, adjusting the oxygen prongs in his nose. Although today was Wednesday, five days after the surgery, Frank was still not off his oxygen. The doctor had assured them yesterday the oxygen was a temporary blip, but it seemed he probably was going home on it.

"I can tell you I'm looking forward to sleeping in my own bed and eating Hannah's cooking again," Frank said. He glanced at Hannah and smiled.

Charlotte couldn't blame him for his eagerness to get home. Each day she visited him he looked paler and paler. It was as if the hospital stay was taking a lot out of him rather than helping him. Charlotte glanced over at Hannah, but her friend stood at the bedside looking down at her hands instead of at her husband.

"And the oxygen?" Charlotte asked.

"Not a problem," Hannah said with a flash of her old self. "The doctor gave me all the instructions. Said it wasn't difficult. He said Frank could stay on it at home until they wean him off."

Charlotte wished she could share Hannah's cavalier attitude, but maybe weaning someone off oxygen actually wasn't that difficult.

"It will be fine," Hannah said with a reassuring tone. Charlotte had to admit she was relieved to see the old Hannah back.

"Did he tell you what needs to be done?" she asked.

"He gave me a pamphlet." Frank reached over to pull a paper off the bedside table, but Hannah took it from him.

"It's nothing onerous. Just basic maintenance."

"Taking care of the oxygen will definitely be an adjustment." Charlotte chose her words carefully, not wanting to make Hannah uncomfortable.

"He said it was only temporary," Hannah said. She looked over at Charlotte. "You don't need to worry about me. It will all be fine."

Frank drew in enough breath to ask Bob a question about the crops and Bob assured him that the neighboring farmers were pitching in to pick up the slack on the Carters' farm. Soon the men were engaged in conversation about rainfall, spraying mixtures, and irrigation problems.

Charlotte glanced at Hannah, now smiling down at Frank. The past few days she'd started to see more of the old Hannah, and today it seemed Hannah was back to her old, capable self. Yet Charlotte couldn't help wonder at the change in her friend. As if it were forced.

"How are you feeling today, Frank?" Charlotte asked.

"Kind of melancholy," he said, turning his head back to Charlotte. "This heart attack has been a real eye-opener for me." With his other hand he fiddled with the sheet covering his chest. "I ... uh ... know I haven't always done what I should. Haven't been as involved in things as I should. I have some regrets."

"What are you talking about?" Bob looked taken aback. "What could you possibly have regrets about?"

Frank released a light laugh. "I've had time during the past few days to think about my life. And what I've done with it." He looked away, as if ashamed. "I feel like I spent my time on the wrong things. Trying to get my farm going. Trying to make sure everything went the way I wanted it to. Now, after coming so close to death, I wish I had spent time on the things that mattered."

Bob frowned. "You have. Your farm is successful, and you've done well."

"From a farmer's point of view." Frank pleated the sheet between his fingers, looking away from Hannah. "I think I should have spent more time with friends and family. Should have spent more time praying." Frank let the sentence drift off and followed it with another sigh. "I regret not taking more time for relationships."

Charlotte wondered if she would feel the same if she had come as close to death as Frank had. She glanced at Bob, who sat hunched over, tapping his fingers together and frowning. Was he wondering the same thing she was?

"We don't need to talk about that now," Hannah said, stroking Frank's hand. "You're here, and you've got lots of life ahead of you."

Bob made a show of looking at his watch. "I guess we should be moving along. I've got to get some parts yet."

"You and I can stay awhile, Hannah, if you want. Bob can pick us up later."

But Hannah bent over and picked up her purse. "I should get going as well. I have a few errands to run before the stores close."

"What errands? Maybe Bob can pick up what you need," Charlotte suggested.

Hannah shook her head. "I, uh, need to get some grocery shopping done."

What could she possibly need at the grocery store? She was staying at their place.

Hannah was already slipping her worn purse over her shoulder and bending over to kiss Frank.

"Then I guess this is good-bye," Charlotte said. She gave Frank a smile. "We'll be praying for you."

"Thanks so much, and thanks for coming." Frank lifted his hand in a wave. Charlotte followed Bob out of the room, giving Hannah a chance to speak to Frank alone.

Bob and Charlotte walked down the hall in silence. A frown creased Bob's face, his hands shoved in the pockets of his jacket. She wondered what he was thinking.

They had only reached the end of the hallway when Hannah caught up to them.

"That was quick," Charlotte said.

"He was tired and needed to rest." Hannah dug into her purse and pulled out a piece of paper. "I'd like to get to the grocery store now, if that's okay."

Charlotte frowned. "What do you need?"

Hannah sighed and then straightened her shoulders. "I've stayed at your place long enough," she said. "I need to go back home and get things ready for Frank."

"But, Hannah, you're just starting to feel better."

"Which is exactly why I should be moving back home. I know I'm welcome to stay as long as I want, but I need to start standing on my own two feet."

"You know you're welcome to stay." Charlotte hesitated, not sure she wanted her friend to be alone. "Are you sure this is what you want?"

"I know what I need," she said firmly. "And it's what you need. You have enough going on in your household."

Charlotte wasn't going to deny that, but she still felt uneasy about letting Hannah go back to her empty house.

"Okay, if you're absolutely sure."

"I am." Hannah gave her a quick smile and then turned around and strode briskly down the hall, as if taking charge of her life once again.

Yet as she and Bob followed, Charlotte couldn't stop a niggling sense of unease.

Something seemed off with her friend. But Charlotte doubted she would find out what that something was until Hannah was ready to tell her.

"ARE YOU STILL hanging around here?"

Uncle Bill's voice boomed from the doorway of the file room, and Sam jumped.

"Yeah. I've just got to finish this filing, and then I'm going home." He had decided to stay late tonight since

Mrs. Pictou had been watching him like a hawk the past two days. As if she were waiting for Bill Stevenson's nephew to mess up.

And of course he *had* made a few mistakes. He gave her a letter that was supposed to go to Lena, Uncle Bill's secretary, even though Mrs. Pictou's name appeared clearly on the letter. He didn't know how he was supposed to have figured that one out. Then Lena gave him a file and he put it in the wrong place; then when she needed it again, he spent most of the morning looking for it.

"I know you've only just started, but how are you enjoying the work so far?" Uncle Bill asked.

Sam wasn't sure what to say. He thought it would be more dramatic. Like on the television shows with trips to the courthouse and people arguing and important errands to run.

"I'm learning lots," he said. Which was partly true. Learning how to make coffee and learning how a filing system in a lawyer's office works. "Moving files around isn't as big a deal as moving irrigation pipes—and it's a whole lot easier."

"Don't downplay the importance of an orderly filing system," Uncle Bill said with a frown that made Sam realize his little joke wasn't appreciated.

"Of course." What else could he say?

"How are things on the farm?" Uncle Bill asked, folding his arms over his chest, like he was settling in for a chat.

So now, Sam guessed, he was going to be Uncle Bill instead of his boss.

Sam hoped he wasn't going to talk long. He had things to do and places to go.

He'd been trying to contact Arielle all day to make plans for tonight, but she wasn't answering her cell phone so he left messages and figured he'd stop by her house after work. He knew she was working at Jenny's tonight but maybe he could meet her late.

"Good, I guess," Sam said. "Grandma hasn't been around much. She's been driving Mrs. Carter back and forth to the hospital to visit with Mr. Carter."

"Is Frank still in the hospital?" Uncle Bill asked.

"Yep, as far as I know." Sam tried hard not to look down at the papers he still had to file. Most of the secretarial staff had gone home already, and he really hoped to catch Arielle.

"I hope he's home soon." Uncle Bill glanced at his watch. "Well, I better get going. I promised Anna I would be home on time for a change. I just thought I'd stop by. Mrs. Pictou told me you had a few mishaps this morning."

"I just put a file in the wrong place. No big deal." Why was she on his case so bad?

Uncle Bill shook his head. "There's no *just* in this office, Sam. We need to be able to find things immediately. Time is always of the essence in a law firm. Cases have been won and lost on the ability to retrieve information quickly."

Sam wanted to protest, but he also wanted to keep the job; the money was good. "I understand," he said. "I'm sorry."

"Good. I'm glad we had this little chat." Uncle Bill tapped the file he held against his leg. "I know there's a lot to learn. I'm sure you'll catch on."

Annoyance tightened his head. It was like Uncle Bill and Mrs. Pictou were waiting for him to mess up.

Don't get smart, he could almost hear Uncle Pete say. So he just nodded and kept his mouth shut.

"Just thought I'd pass that on. You have a good evening." Uncle Bill set the file in the basket and strode away.

Sam sighed. He really thought this job would be more interesting and important when he took it. He thought he might be visiting the court, delivering files, listening in on important cases. But in reality he was just a file clerk and coffee person.

He stayed a bit longer, just to make sure he'd gotten everything right, and when he was satisfied, he left.

On his way home, he tried calling Arielle again on his cell phone, but his call went right to her voice mail. He tried her home number but got the answering machine. He made a quick decision and turned down the road to her house. She was supposed to be his girlfriend, but they hadn't seen each other all week. Sure, they had both started new jobs, but that was no reason to be avoiding each other. As he pulled up, he was surprised to see her old truck parked in the driveway.

If she's home, why isn't she answering the telephone? Sam wondered.

He knocked on the door. Then again. Finally the door opened, and Arielle answered. Her hair was all messy, and she wore a robe over pajamas. Her eyes were all red.

"Sam. Hey." She sounded funny.

"Are you okay? I thought you were at work," he said, pulling open the door.

"Yeah. I left a little early." She yawned.

"You sure you're okay? You look kind of sick."

"Thanks—I think," she said with a little laugh. "No, I was just lying down."

"Oh." Sam felt puzzled. "I tried to call you."

"I turned my phone off. I didn't sleep well last night. In fact, I didn't sleep at all."

"Why not?"

Arielle pulled her bathrobe closer and then shrugged. "I guess I just have a lot on my mind. What with college and all."

"You're not going to college for over a month," he said, hoping to reassure her. "You don't need to start stressing already."

Arielle gave him a quick smile. "No. I suppose not. I tend to worry, that's all."

He stroked her shoulder. Then he reached up to tuck her hair behind her ear, but she pulled away. "I'm getting worried about you. You've seemed distant."

"Just tired and stressed." Arielle stifled a yawn.

"Okay, I get the hint. I'm leaving now. I just thought I'd stop by..." He didn't know what else to say. He didn't want to make her feel guilty by telling her he'd hoped to go out with her tonight. Unless she'd already checked her messages and already knew.

"Thanks, Sam. That was sweet." She looked up, gave him a quick smile, and then took a step away.

"I'll...uh...let you get back to bed then." Sam wanted to give her a hug, but the way she was acting, he figured she'd just pull away again. "Take care. I'll call you tomorrow. Maybe we can make some plans for the weekend."

"The weekend. Sure. We'll see."

He took a chance and gave her a quick kiss and then closed the door. But as he got into his car, he looked over at the house. Arielle stood at the living room window, watching him. She wasn't smiling.

As he drove away, he sighed. Things were off between them. They'd been through that before when they broke up awhile back, but he thought they'd been on pretty solid footing lately.

He shook off the feeling. Guess he was free tonight. Maybe Jake was too.

Jake was locking the door of the video store when Sam pulled up.

"Hey, man, what's up?" Jake asked as he dropped the keys into his pocket.

"Just wondering if you wanted to split a pizza with me. Arielle's sick, and I don't feel like going home."

"Why don't you come with me? I'm meeting Kelsey at a cottage her parents own on the lake. I was just heading out to pick up some pizza too. You could totally hang with us."

"If that's okay."

"It'd be cool to spend some time together." Jake spun the keys around his finger. "Why don't you follow me?"

"Paul coming?"

"Nah. He's got some army thing he has to go to. But it will still be fun."

"Yeah. Sure. Sounds good." At least the day wasn't going to be a total loss. He phoned home, got the answering machine, and left a message saying he wasn't coming home for supper.

Ten minutes later he was following Jake up a winding

road. He caught the occasional glimpse of cottages and houses through breaks in the thick trees. He'd never been up this road before. Jake's taillights flashed, and then his car turned into a paved driveway. Sam was glad he was following his buddy. He never would have found the place himself.

Jake pulled up behind a couple of cars and a bright, red pickup truck that reminded Sam of his dad's. Looked like some other people were here already.

He got out of the car, looking around. *Some cottage*, he thought, looking over the two-story wooden structure perched on a hill surrounded by trees. It was built in an A-frame style, and the entire front of the building, overlooking the lake, was one expanse of glass. A deck extended from the lower floor, and a couple of kids were leaning on its railing, laughing and chatting.

From inside the house, music pounded out a techno beat. It didn't seem like Mr. and Mrs. Vance, Kelsey's parents, were here.

"Hey, Jake," Kelsey called out, leaning way over the railing, her wet hair hanging down. "Is that Sam you got there?"

"Yeah. I figured we needed some help demolishing all the pizza you ordered," Jake answered as he opened the back door of his car. "You must be expecting all of Bedford to come?"

"Nope," Kelsey replied. "Just you and your buddies."

Jake handed Sam four large pizza boxes, the bottoms warm and greasy from the pizza inside. "Take these up to the house, and you'll be the most popular guy here. I'll get the pop and chips."

Sam laughed as he headed up the gravel path to the house. He recognized a couple of the guys hanging out on the deck. He'd had Wilson in his chem class and Artie in his English class. Wilson was always good for a laugh and always had a joke or two in class. Aunt Dana didn't care for him, but Sam thought he was okay.

The other guy standing with Artie and Wilson was unfamiliar.

"Sam, my man," Wilson called out above the music. "Great to see you here. Thanks for the pizza." He grabbed the boxes and then glanced around, looking puzzled. "What are the rest of you going to eat?"

"Very funny," Kelsey yelled back from inside the kitchen. "Bring them into the kitchen, and we'll divvy them up."

"Hey, Kels. Can we turn the stereo down?" Jake said, raising his voice to be heard above the music.

"Yeah. Sorry. We were outside and couldn't hear it."

Jake dropped a kiss on Kelsey's head. "Gotta watch that, girl. Don't want the neighbors complaining."

"Those neighbors complain about every little thing," Kelsey said with a shrug.

"Maybe we can give them a big thing to complain about," Wilson said with a grin. "Make it worth their while."

Artie and the unfamiliar guy laughed about this, but Sam just smiled. He felt funny being in this place with Kelsey's parents gone, but hey, he didn't want to ruin the party.

"How long are your parents gone for?" Wilson asked, flipping open the top of the pizza box.

"Me and my sis have this place to ourselves for two

wonderful weeks while Mom and Dad are driving cross-country to California," Kelsey said with a laugh, spreading her arms wide.

Wilson pulled a large triangle of pizza out of the box and took a bite. "So we can hang here until then?" he mumbled around a mouthful of pizza.

"No. You can't. Not unless you're invited," Kelsey said, wagging a playful finger at him.

"Who else did you ask?" Jake asked, craning his head to look out the window as he dropped another box on the table.

Kelsey looked out the window as well and groaned. "Oh, that's just my sister's boyfriend and some of his buddies."

More people filed in, more food arrived, and the noise level increased.

An hour later Sam was feeling better. One of the girls he had just met was flirting with him, which seemed weird, but at the same time made him feel less annoyed about Arielle putting him off.

Later, he turned down an opportunity to go swimming, figuring he had better head home. He was still plenty early for his curfew, but he didn't want to push things too hard.

"You sure you gotta go?" Wilson asked, flinging an arm over his shoulder. "We're just starting to have fun."

"Yeah. I've got to help on the farm tomorrow," Sam said.

"That's cool," Wilson said, seeming to mean it. "I wish I lived on a farm. I get tired of living in town. You got horses?"

"Yeah."

"Wow. Lucky guy." Wilson slapped him on the back.

"We'll be hanging out here a lot so you'll have to come again."

"Of course he'll come," Kelsey called out. "He's Jake's best buddy."

"Now he's ours too." Artie raised his can of pop as if toasting Sam. "You better show up, Sam. I've got to redeem myself. Never been beat at my own card game."

Sam laughed, a sense of well-being washing over him. "Yeah. Sure. I'll hang out again."

He drove home, whistling all the way and thinking that things had turned out okay after all.

Chapter Eleven

"So that's chapel for this Wednesday night." Pastor Jason, the leader for the evening, announced from the stage at the front of the auditorium. The band stood behind him, waiting to play. Mike stood behind Jason, his hands folded over the top of his electric guitar, his long hair hanging over his eyes. He shook it back, looked out over the audience, and caught Emily's eye.

Emily felt a peculiar jolt and then quickly looked away. *This is weird*, she thought. Then she pushed the feelings aside. She missed Troy—that was all. And there was no way to get in touch with him because no one had a cell phone and the line at the only phone the campers could use was always too long. Besides, the phone was only available from noon to five o'clock.

"Our worship band will play one last song, and then it's campfire time."

Emily glanced around the auditorium. The benches were placed in a semicircle facing the stage. The floor was cement and always dusty. No one was dressed up. Everyone wore hoodies or T-shirts and jeans. Most everyone seemed to be having a good time. The energy in the gathering gave her a shiver.

"I don't feel like going to campfire," Ashley whispered to Emily just as Jason stepped aside for the band. "I didn't get enough sleep last night."

"I told you to stop talking," Emily said with a laugh.

"I know. It didn't help that Nicole wouldn't stop either."

"I know what you mean." Having Nicole in their cabin was a definite downer. She and Ashley had to be careful what they talked about, which wasn't as much fun.

"We'll have to find someplace we can talk away from her," Ashley said. "She's starting to get to me." Ashley yawned again as the drummer started a quick beat. The guitars joined in, and soon the campers were on their feet, the scrape of the wooden benches on the floor barely heard above the noise of the band. "You coming back to the cabin with me?" Ashley asked, raising her voice to be heard.

Emily shot a quick glance at the front of the auditorium. Mike stood on the stage, singing, his head bent over his guitar as if lost in the music.

Ever since she had seen him on the dock the first day she was here, Emily had been looking out for him. It was as if he had disappeared. Then, the second night in the auditorium, a tall figure sauntered up to the stage. Her heart did a funny little flip when she saw Mike pick up a guitar and sling it over his shoulder.

She had a boyfriend, she kept reminding herself. A guy she really liked. Yet something about Mike caught her attention.

Emily shook her head. "I'm not tired," she yelled back, dragging her attention back to Ashley.

Ashley was grinning at her. "Or you want to see if Mike is coming to campfire?" she said in Emily's ear.

A flush warmed her cheeks. "I like campfire," she said, thankful this was the truth.

"I know you do," Ashley said, tucking her arm through Emily's. "Just kidding. But I'm gonna go back to the cabin. See you later." Though the band still played, Ashley snuck out. Emily joined in the song, glad she remembered some of the words.

When the music was over though, she felt a bit lost without Ashley at her side. She hung back, watching as the rest of the kids drifted out of the auditorium, the buzz of their conversation filling the air.

She glanced back at the stage. Mike was packing up his guitar. She hesitated and then turned and followed the other kids through the double doors and down a well-worn path to the campfire pit.

The fire was already snapping and crackling by the time Emily got there. Some kids were already sitting on the benches surrounding the fire. Emily chose an old tree stump that wasn't too close so it gave her some privacy.

Campfire was a chance for people to talk about some of the things they had experienced during the day, some lesson or spiritual insight.

"Hey, Emily." One of the girls she and Ashley had gone canoeing with sat down on the dirt beside her. She had short, spiky hair and an earring in her eyebrow. Emily tried to imagine herself coming home looking like that. Grandma would have a fit. "Nice weather, huh?" the girl asked.

"I know. I was going to wear my hoodie, but I'm glad I didn't."

"You wanna sit closer to the fire?"

"I'm okay." Sitting closer meant she would be closer to the leader. She was fine where she was, especially if Ashley wasn't around.

The noise level got higher as more kids joined the circle.

Then the leader arrived, and things quieted down. Colette was a short, slender woman with long, blonde hair pulled back in a ponytail. Emily had spent the morning with her making crafts and had gotten to know her pretty well.

"I'd like to try something different tonight," Colette shouted out, getting everyone's attention. "I thought we could do a question period. I'll throw out a question, and the first person to answer it gets to throw out another question, and we'll just keep going like that. Game?"

"Is that the question?" someone called out. Emily recognized Harley, a tall, slightly overweight young man who was a lot of fun.

"What do you think?" she returned.

"I think that's the question. And I just answered it. Now I get to ask something." Harley jumped up and stuck his hands in the back pockets of his blue jeans, his face shining in the glow of the fire. "My question is, why can't we have shorter weeks and longer weekends?"

"Because God only rested on the Sabbath," someone called out from the opposite side of the fire. Emily recognized Nicole's voice.

"That's no answer," Harley said.

"It's the right answer," Nicole returned. "Now it's my turn." She stood up and looked around. Through the flickering flames, it seemed as if her gaze rested on Emily. "My question is, why can't people be nicer to each other?"

Was Nicole accusing her?

Emily's ears burned, and once again she was thankful she was sitting back, away from the fire. There was no way she would even take a breath; she didn't want anyone to think she was ready to answer that question.

"Because we're only human." Emily was relieved when someone answered the question right away. It was another girl. "So why don't we want to serve God better?"

Emily squirmed, trying to make herself smaller and insignificant. She had figured people would be asking silly questions, not getting all philosophical.

"Getting kinda heavy, isn't it?"

Emily jumped and spun around just as Mike appeared out of the darkness behind her.

"Sorry," he said, touching her arm lightly. His eyes glowed in the reflected firelight. "I thought you heard me come up."

"I didn't," she whispered, keeping her voice low, hoping he wouldn't hear how shaky she sounded.

Mike dropped down to the ground beside her and pulled his knees up to his chest. "Again. Sorry." He shot her a quick glance and then looked over at the gathered group. "I missed the last two campfires; is it always this deep?"

Emily waited for her heart to settle down, angry with herself for her reaction to him. What was wrong with her? She had a boyfriend, for goodness' sake. A boyfriend she thought she would miss. A lot.

"Yesterday we played some game about packing a suitcase, so I guess not."

"That sounds like more fun." He sighed and leaned back. "So, you still enjoying camp?"

"Yeah. I am. People are really nice, and there's lots of stuff to do. I went canoeing yesterday and had a blast." She hadn't seen him there, though most of the other kids of their age group had gone. "I didn't see you there." As soon as the words left her mouth, Emily felt like smacking herself on the head. Great. Now she sounded like she was flirting with him.

"I dunno. I'm not much of a canoer."

"I was nervous at first but got used to it," Emily said, feeling funny that she was trying to reassure him. He seemed so confident. So able.

"I've been in canoes before," he said. "I used to go lots until . . ." He stopped there. Then he made a sound that might have been a laugh but sounded more like a snort. "Sorry. That slipped out."

She wondered what he meant by his comment, but the angry look on his face made her decide to change the subject.

"How about the horses? Did you ever ride here?" Emily asked instead.

"I have, but I ride at home too. My dad raises quarter-horse-Morgan crossbreeds." He glanced sidelong at her. "What about you? Do you ride?"

"We've got a few horses on our farm. I ride when I can." Which wasn't as often as she knew she should, but she did enjoy it when she went out.

"What kind of horses do you have?"

Emily shrugged, wishing she could remember, but she

knew she couldn't fake it. "Let's see, we have a brown one, a black-and-brown one, a mostly brown one..."

Mike laughed at her dumb answer.

"Sorry," she said with a quick grin. "My uncle raises them, and even he's not sure of the breeding."

"Do your parents go riding?"

Emily pressed her hands together, trying to figure out the best way to explain the situation without looking like she was angling for sympathy.

"My dad left my mom when I was about five. He comes by once in a while now, but we're not real close. And my mother..." To Emily's surprise and embarrassment, her throat thickened with tears. She hadn't cried about her mother in months. Now, in front of a virtual stranger, and a cute virtual stranger at that, she was starting to get all choked up. She took a quick breath and forged on. "My mother died in a car accident about two years ago now."

She swallowed and then chanced a quick look at Mike, but he was staring at the fire, the flickering orange flames lighting up his face one second and darkening it the next.

Then he looked at her, and she saw it again. A flash of deep pain in his eyes. And was that a glimmer of tears or a trick of the fire?

"It's hard, isn't it?" he asked. Then he looked quickly away as the atmosphere shifted and changed. His quiet question made her wonder.

Emily leaned closer to him and kept her voice low and quiet.

"Did you lose your mother too?"

Mike clenched his hands into fists, his lips pressed together.

"Let's go for a walk," he said, pushing himself to his feet.

Emily hesitated just a moment, but the pain in his voice called to the pain in her own life. She got up as well.

Mike headed toward the beach, and she followed him there, struggling through the soft sand to keep up with his long-legged stride. He slowed down but said nothing as they walked side by side, neither saying a word. He turned toward the dock, the same place she had seen him the first time she had come here.

Their footsteps echoed on the wooden planks, their weight creating a faint sloshing of water against the sides of the dock. A softly lit moon hung just above the hills surrounding the lake, giving the water an ethereal glow.

Mike stopped at the end, looking out over the water, his hands in the pockets of his blue jeans. They stood in silence for a few more minutes as the water lapped against the wood, creating a quiet, hypnotic sound.

"Ten months ago my mother drowned."

"Oh, no! I'm so sorry," Emily breathed.

"She was in a canoe. I was following her. I couldn't get to her in time." He stopped there, his hands clenched at his side.

Emily tried to keep herself apart from the anger in his voice, recognizing, in some small way, the anger she had struggled with herself.

The difference was that she hadn't witnessed her mother's death.

He turned to her, his eyes glittering in the moonlight. "Sometimes I hate God. Sometimes I hate myself because I couldn't save her."

She just stared at him, not sure what to say.

"I know I shouldn't say that at a Bible camp, but that's how I feel. If you can't handle that, you can just leave," he said.

Emily held his gaze, easily remembering the anger that overtook her after her mother's death. "I don't need to handle it," she said, trying to find exactly the right words. "I just want to listen."

Mike's shoulders lowered, and his hands slowly uncurled. Then, as if all the fight had slipped out of him, he lowered himself to the dock, sitting cross-legged on the damp wood, his arms resting on his knees, his hands dangling.

Emily sat down as well, pulling her knees close to her chest. The cool breeze coming off the water felt wonderful after the heat of the day.

"My pastor said I shouldn't feel that way." Mike's voice had lost that angry edge, and he seemed to be sighing the words. "It's not a fun emotion, being so angry all the time. I just don't know where to put it."

"Anger is one of the stages of grieving. At least that's what my grandma told me when me and my brothers moved to the farm after my mom died," Emily said, remembering some of the talks she'd had with Grandma, sitting on her bed. The move from San Diego to the farm had been hard enough to deal with. Moving away from the only place she'd had any memories of her mother had been even more difficult.

But since then her memory bank had been enriched by stories of her mother that Uncle Pete, Uncle Bill, Grandma, and Grandpa had shared with her and her brothers.

"That's what the counselor told me too." Mike stretched his hands out in front of him. "He told me I was probably projecting my anger about my mother's death toward myself. I didn't believe him, so I stopped going to counseling."

Emily just shrugged, still not sure of where she was going, but she thought of her own feelings. "I think you always feel guilty when someone you know dies. Especially if you were right there. I can't imagine what that must have been like for you."

Mike said nothing, and Emily knew he needed the quiet. Finally she asked him, "How was your dad about this all?"

"He cried a lot. Got angry." Mike brought his hands behind him and leaned back. "We rode the horses a lot. Dad figured that was just as good a therapy as seeing a counselor."

Emily remembered how she had spent time with Britney and Stormy, her mother's horse and her newborn foal, the first few weeks after they moved to the farm. "The horses kind of take you as you are, don't they?" Emily said.

Mike laughed again, but this time it sounded softer. Happier. "Do you miss her?"

Emily knew exactly what he was talking about. "Lots."

"Does it go away? The pain?"

Emily tested that thought as she pulled up a memory of her mother and then shook her head slowly. "Not really, but it does get easier. And there comes a time when the memories can make you smile instead of cry."

"You were almost crying by the fire."

Emily hugged her knees a bit harder. "I think that's because seeing your pain made me remember how it felt. But only for a while. I'm not crying anymore."

Mike didn't say anything in reply, which was fine with

Emily. She was more than content to just sit there, looking out over the lake, the gentle lapping of the waves soothing away the remnants of her own pain. She felt a peace she hadn't known in a long, long time. Mike understood what she had dealt with. She could talk to him in a way she hadn't been able to talk to anyone since her mom died.

Ashley was a good friend, and though she had recently had her own scare with her mother's cancer, Melody Givens was still around and still alive. Ashley didn't truly understand what it was like to lose a mom.

Grandma and Grandpa had been upset themselves, and Emily tried not to talk too much about her own sadness because she was afraid it would make things worse for them. So sometimes it was hard to be honest.

But Mike knew. He got it.

Mike lay back on the dock, looking up; Emily dropped her head back to look up at the stars as well. Laughter from the people around the campfire drifted over the water toward them, but it was softened by the distance. It was as if the two of them were in their own space.

He rolled over to his side, propping his head up on his elbow. "Do you have a boyfriend?"

Emily kept her face toward the night sky, her cheeks flushing at his abrupt question. Part of her wanted to say no, but she knew that wasn't fair to Troy. "Yes. I do."

"I have a girlfriend back home."

Did she feel just a brush of disappointment?

"I like it that we can just talk together," he continued. "That we can be friends without all that other stuff that can come between guys and girls."

Emily let that comment settle a moment and then

realized he was right. All her friends were girls, except for Hunter, who sometimes rode horses with her. It was nice to know someone like Mike could be just a friend.

"I think it's cool too," she said, shooting him a quick smile. The breeze coming off the lake picked up, and she shivered again. "I'm going back to the fire because now I'm getting cold."

Mike jumped to his feet, pulling his jacket off. "Sorry. I wasn't thinking. I should have offered you my coat."

"That's okay," Emily said, standing up. "I guess I'll see you around."

"Yeah. I guess. Hey, do you mind if we do this another time?"

He has a girlfriend. You have a boyfriend. The words echoed in her mind. At the same time, she experienced a kinship with him that she hadn't felt with anyone else. Not even Ashley.

"No. I don't mind at all."

"Great. See you tomorrow night then. After worship."

Emily nodded. Then, hugging herself against a sudden chill, she walked back across the dock. She bypassed the fire and went straight to her cabin. When she slipped through the door, she heard Ashley's gentle snoring flowing from the top bunk, and relief flowed through her. Though she and Mike had done nothing wrong, she still wanted to guard the moment. And she didn't really want to talk to Ashley about it.

Emily brushed her teeth and washed up; then she crawled into her sleeping bag on her bed. She folded her hands over her chest as she stared up at the top bunk. She thought of Troy and smiled, glad to know she missed him. A bit.

The door creaked open. "Emily, are you in there?"

Her heart dropped. What was Nicole doing back from campfire already? She wanted to pretend to be asleep but knew Nicole had probably seen her walking past, heading to the cabin.

"Yeah. I am."

The door creaked shut, and Nicole walked over to Emily's bunk and sat down at the end. Just as if she were settling in for a little heart-to-heart chat.

"I saw you with that Mike guy."

Nicole sounded like she had other things on her mind. Knowing Nicole, it would probably not be good. "Yeah, I'm sure you did."

"He's cute. You guys seemed kind of cozy." Nicole sounded like she was fishing for more information. Emily figured she'd better stop this right away. No sense in giving Nicole any reason to start any rumors.

"He has a girlfriend, and I have a boyfriend." Hopefully that was the end of that. "We just talked."

"Of course." But in the pale light coming in the cabin from outside, Emily caught Nicole's expression.

It didn't look good.

Chapter Twelve

"I think Frank and I should take a trip. What do you think? I've always wanted to go to the Caribbean," Hannah said over the sizzle of stew meat she was browning in the frying pan.

"Where do you keep the chopping knife?" Charlotte asked, pulling open one of the drawers in Hannah's kitchen.

"In the block," Hannah said, motioning with her chin.

"Why do you want to go to the Caribbean?" Charlotte asked as she started chopping the carrots she had just washed.

Frank was coming home tomorrow, and Charlotte had gone to Hannah's house to help get some meals ready so Hannah would have less on her mind his first few days back.

"I've always wanted to go," Hannah said. "Frank and I have been saving up for a trip for years. Maybe we should go this year."

Charlotte tried to imagine Hannah and Frank ambling down the beaches of Aruba or Bermuda. "Might be a little tricky with Frank being on oxygen," was all she said.

"We could manage." Hannah transferred the meat into the Crock-Pot sitting on the counter.

"He might not like that too much," Charlotte said with a light laugh. She was glad to see her friend making some plans, looking so chipper. Today she looked much happier. She had combed her hair, put on some makeup, and was wearing one of her favorite sweatshirts. She seemed genuinely happy to be in her own home, and tomorrow she wouldn't be sleeping here alone.

Hannah sighed, picking up the salt container, shaking it vigorously.

"You might want to hold back a bit on the salt," Charlotte said, looking up from chopping the carrots. "You know what the doctor said about that."

"Of course," Hannah said with a bright tone. "How could I forget?"

Charlotte put her hand on her friend's arm. "Are you sure you're okay? I could arrange for some of the women from the church to come and stay with you. Keep you company."

Hannah snorted. "I'm not that feeble, especially now that I'm feeling so much better. I can manage."

Charlotte couldn't deny that. Hannah was always so capable.

Hannah flashed Charlotte a smile. "I can tell you don't believe me."

"Well, it *is* a lot to deal with—Frank's brush with death, and now he's coming home on oxygen." To Charlotte it seemed a big responsibility.

"He'll be off it in no time," Hannah assured her.

Charlotte wasn't as sure as her friend was, but Hannah had spent more time with the therapists than she had, so she wasn't about to argue with her.

They worked in silence awhile, and Charlotte couldn't

help an occasional glance at the clock. She had work to get back to, but she also wanted to be a support to her friend.

Finally Hannah turned to Charlotte and spun her around. "It's time you go home," she said, untying Charlotte's apron with brisk, decisive movements. "I can manage just fine, and I know you have lots to do."

Hannah was right. She did have a lot to do.

Hannah put her hands on Charlotte's shoulders. "Don't worry about me. I'm a tough woman. Frank and I will get through this."

"I know, but you are also allowed to let people help you."

Hannah waved away her comment. "I told you. I'm fine. Frank and I will manage just fine." She gave Charlotte a bright smile as if to underline her vociferous statement. Then she gave her a gentle push toward the door. "Now go back to your family. They need you too."

Charlotte hesitated a moment, not completely convinced her friend was as fine as she said she was.

But what could she do or say? She had given Hannah every opportunity to accept her help, and if Hannah said she was fine, then Charlotte had to believe her. So she folded up her apron and left.

But all the way home, she couldn't shake the feeling that something wasn't quite right.

"I CAN'T BELIEVE it's Friday already," Ashley said from the back of the canoe. "It seems like we just got here."

"I can't believe how warm it is," Emily put the paddle on the bottom of the canoe and pulled off her life jacket so she could take off her hoodie. The sun beat down on her head and glinted off the water of the lake. She was getting hot.

She and Ashley were trying to keep up with the group that was supposed to be on a lakeshore scavenger hunt. Eight canoes had set out from the dock an hour ago, two people per canoe. Each team had a list of things they were supposed to find. The team with the most checkmarks won.

Emily wasn't that good in the canoe yet, so she and Ashley had fallen behind. Because they were now in a cove, the rest of the canoes were obscured by the tall, thick cattails growing along the lakeshore that they were trying to paddle around.

"I told you you should have brought a hat instead of using your hood," Ashley said from her seat at the back of the canoe.

"Probably should have, but..." Emily stopped, standing up so she could put her folded hoodie under her on the canoe's seat. Right now it would be better used as a cushion than as clothing.

"You didn't want to mess up your hair."

Emily tossed a quick glance over her shoulder, making the canoe rock a bit. Ashley was grinning back at her. "Well, yeah."

"No sense keeping your hair nice if Mike can't even see it. He's way ahead by now."

"It's not like that," Emily said, hoping Ashley would think her blush had more to do with how hot she was than with being self-conscious.

"I know. I'm just kidding you."

Emily had told Ashley about Mike and what had happened, and to her relief Ashley didn't think it was weird at all. In fact, she had encouraged Emily to talk to Mike. To let him know she understood what it was like to lose a mother.

When he found out she and Ashley were going canoeing, he said he was coming too. Which surprised Emily and, if she were honest, gave her a little thrill of excitement, although she was worried that Nicole might stir up trouble if she saw the two of them together.

"We'll never catch up with the rest of them," Emily said before sitting down again and picking up her paddle.

"At least we got some of the stuff on our list," Ashley said. "Now we need to see a lake trout."

"I don't even know what a trout looks like," Emily said, dipping her paddle in the cool water. "And how do they know we even saw one? I mean, we could just lie about it and say we did. What if the other teams are doing the same thing?"

She reached farther and then pulled her paddle through the water. Though she wasn't any good at it, she did love the peace and quiet of canoeing. The only sound was the drip of water and the faint sloshing against the side of their boat.

"It says here that we need to describe the fish, so if you've never seen one before, you might get caught."

"Are you helping back there, or are you reading?" Emily asked, grunting as she paddled.

"Sorry." Their canoe suddenly shot ahead as Ashley joined in. They came out around the cattails, and suddenly another canoe appeared in front of them.

Emily blushed again.

Mike was manning the front of the canoe while Scott, another camper, was in the back. Had he heard what she and Ashley were talking about a moment ago? She hoped not.

"Aren't you going the wrong way?" Ashley called out.

"Our fearless leader sent us out to look for you," Mike said, frowning at Emily. "He figured for sure you guys had dumped your canoe."

"Hey, we're not totally clueless," Emily said.

Mike stared at her for a second, but then he relaxed. "But you *are* totally behind," Mike said.

"We can catch up. In fact, we'll pass you."

"I doubt that, missy," Mike said. "I've canoed for years."

"Doesn't matter; we've got heart and spirit, right Ashley?" Emily glanced back at Ashley, who nodded, acknowledging her dare. Ashley dug her paddle into the water. Emily started up again, reaching forward with every stroke and pulling for all she was worth. They started moving ahead of the other canoe.

"Keep going! You're doing great," Scott said from behind them.

"We're getting ahead," Ashley called out.

Emily kept paddling, ignoring the sweat trickling down her back as she worked harder than she had ever worked. The other canoes had stopped, and soon she and Ashley were closing in on them.

"Pull. Pull. Pull. Pull," Mike called, as if keeping time for them. "Ramming speed. Pull. Pull."

Emily started to laugh. She switched her paddle to the other side.

Suddenly the canoe tipped sideways.

Emily watched in horror as the water surged toward her, and then she was in it. The cold water washed over her, the sudden shock making her gasp, but her face was submerged, and she sucked in a mouthful of water.

She couldn't breathe. She didn't know which way was

up as she spun around trying to find the surface in the cold water. She couldn't move. To her horror she realized she had gotten tangled in the weeds. Strands pulled at her feet and tangled in her hair, keeping her down. Panic clawed at her chest. She was going to die.

Then a hand grasped her arm and pulled. She felt herself being yanked sideways—or what she thought was sideways as she was pulled free from the clutches of the weeds and into the light. She broke the surface, water streaming down her face and into her eyes. She tried to pull precious air into her lungs but coughed instead. Then again.

Strong hands held her steady as she flailed around, trying to breathe.

"Emily! Emily!" she heard Ashley's panicked voice call out.

"It's okay. Just relax. It's okay." Mike spoke reassuringly as she clung blindly to him.

Emily coughed again, and blessed air was pulled into her lungs. Which made her cough again. And then another pull of air. More coughing. More air.

Then finally she was breathing normally. Well, not normally perhaps, but steadily.

As her senses reoriented, she opened her eyes and looked into Mike's concerned face, also dripping with water, and relief surged through her. He was treading water and holding her so her head was above the water, and she realized what had just happened.

Even worse, what could have happened had he not been there.

"You saved my life," she said.

"Not really," he protested.

"No. Really." Emily tried to find the bottom with her

feet. "I was stuck in the weeds. If you hadn't pulled me free I wouldn't have come up."

The reality of what might have happened suddenly hit her, and she had to fight the urge to cry.

"You did. You saved my life." Her voice got all trembly—from shock, she figured. Shock and relief.

"Are you okay? Is she okay?"

Emily turned around to see Ashley treading water beside her, her hair soaking wet, her expression one of terror mixed with relief. "You scared the living daylights out of me, Emily!"

"I'm sorry." Emily coughed again. "I'm so sorry."

"Is everyone okay?" The voice of their camp leader, Chris, echoed across the water.

Scott paddled around so he came between Mike and the leader's approaching canoe. "Give this to her right now," he said softly but urgently. He handed Mike the life jacket he had grabbed out of Ashley and Emily's abandoned canoe. "We'll be in major trouble if they find out she wasn't wearing it when she tipped."

Emily felt suddenly foolish. "I forgot to put it back on after I took off my hoodie," she said as she struggled to get into it, no easy feat in water over her head. Mike had to help her do it, but by the time the counselor arrived, the life jacket's clasps were securely snapped, and Emily was able to float away from Mike.

"What happened?" Chris asked as he came alongside Scott. "Is everyone okay?"

"Emily and Ashley tipped—"

"I forgot to say 'change' when I started paddling on the other side." Emily cut Mike off, brushing her wet hair back from her face. "It was my fault."

She wasn't about to tell the counselor what had really happened. Or how close she had come to drowning. She didn't want to face that yet. The horror was too fresh.

She was alive. Mike had saved her.

"Well, as long as everyone is okay, let's get everyone back in the canoe so we can carry on."

A few moments later, with Chris's help, Ashley and Emily were safely back in their canoe, and Mike was back in his.

In spite of the heat of the day, Emily shivered. She didn't want to dwell on what had just happened, or what a close call she'd just had. Instead she looked over at Mike paddling alongside her, looking serious. He caught her look and gave her a crooked smile. "You sure you're okay?"

"I'm sure. Thanks again. That was scary."

"It was." Mike looked away. "It really was."

Emily knew from the tone of his voice that he was thinking about his mother.

"HOW MANY TIMES do we have to go over this? It's the last day of your first week of work and you still can't seem to get things straight." Mrs. Pictou tossed a file onto the desk in the file room, glaring at Sam. "Any correspondence dealing with mortgages and wills goes directly to me."

Sam picked up the file, glanced inside, and frowned. "The letter is addressed to Bill Stevenson."

He looked up just in time to catch the narrowing of her eyes. He knew Mrs. Pictou didn't like him; he just wished he knew why.

"Mr. Stevenson," she corrected, pulling her red-lipsticked mouth tight, like she'd just eaten a lemon.

"Sorry."

"Don't let it happen again." Mrs. Pictou smoothed a hand over her hair and then folded her arms over her chest. "I hope I don't need to speak to Mr. Stevenson about your work."

Sam's heart sank. The last thing he needed was Mrs. Prissy Pictou tattling on him again. He stifled a sigh and forced a smile. "I don't think so." He didn't know what else to say. He would just have to work extra hard.

Mrs. Pictou tapped her fingers against her arm and then spun around on her high heel and left.

Sam let out a sigh. He was trying. He really was. The work wasn't fantastic, and it wasn't as exciting as he'd hoped, but he needed the money.

Fifteen minutes later he had all the mail opened and, he hoped, sorted the right way. He double-checked everything, making sure it was right, and then stepped out of the door of the mail room in time to see Uncle Bill standing in the door of his office listening to Mrs. Pictou.

Great. Just perfect. He ducked back into the room, waiting while bits and pieces of the conversation came back to him.

"If I'd known you were hiring, I know way more capable people than Sam..."

Sam felt a jolt at the few words he heard. It sounded as if Mrs. Pictou had someone else in mind for his job. His hands tightened on the files. Sure, he'd made some mistakes, but he wasn't a complete loser.

He waited a moment and then stuck his head out of the doorway. They were gone. He walked to Lena's desk and handed her the mail.

She smiled up at him as she took it. "Thanks, Sam."

Sam just nodded and glanced back over his shoulder. He couldn't see Mrs. Pictou or his uncle.

"Is Mr. Stevenson around?" he asked, trying to sound innocent. He kind of wanted to know more about what he and Mrs. Pictou had been discussing.

"You mean your Uncle Bill?" Lena said with a laugh.

Sam gave her a puzzled look. "Mrs. Pictou told me I had to call him Mr. Stevenson."

Lena flopped her hand at him. "That's just silly."

"She seemed to think it was pretty important," Sam said.

This netted him another flap of her hand. "Don't worry about Mrs. Pictou."

That was easy for Lena to say. He glanced over his shoulder again, looking for Mrs. Pictou, and then realized he was just being paranoid. If he really wanted this job, he was just going to have to prove to Mrs. Pictou and his uncle that he was worth hiring—and keeping. That he was just as capable as whoever it was Mrs. Pictou had in mind.

He stayed a bit longer that night, neatening up the file cabinets, replacing some of the tattered file folders; as a result he was one of the last ones out of the office.

He tried to call Arielle, but again his call to her cell phone went to voice mail, and his call to her home phone went to the answering machine. Then he tried Jake but got his voice mail too. Paul was busy.

As soon as he pressed the END button from calling Paul, the cell phone immediately rang.

"Hey, there," he said, glancing over his shoulder as he changed lanes. "Who is this?"

"It's Wilson, my man. Remember?"

"I sure do," Sam said. He'd had a lot of fun with Wilson

the other night at the cabin, but at the same time, he didn't think he wanted to spend much more time with Wilson and his friends. Things hadn't gotten out of hand the last time he'd been with them. Not quite. But he knew for sure that Arielle wouldn't approve of Wilson, Artie, and their friends.

"You want to come up tonight? To the cabin?"

"No. I've got a date with my girlfriend," he said, smiling at the thought.

"Too bad. Well, if your plans change, come on over. We've always got room for one more."

"Will Jake be there?"

"Nah. Him and Kelsey have a date too, but she said we're welcome to hang out at the cabin."

"Must be something in the air," Sam said with a quick laugh. "I better go."

Sam shook his head as he clicked his cell phone shut. Given the choice, he'd way rather spend time with Arielle.

He had her home number on speed dial and hit the button. Though he had told Wilson that he and Arielle had a date, they had only made tentative plans for tonight. Sam wanted to take her out to a nice restaurant for dinner. He'd gotten his first week's paycheck already and was feeling pretty flush. He'd never made that much money before.

He called Arielle's cell number again but again she didn't answer. What was up with that? He tried her friend's place, but again, no joy. He knew she wasn't working at Jenny's tonight.

Where could she be?

He tossed his phone on the seat beside him, bummed that he was heading back to the farm on a Friday night when it seemed everyone, including his girlfriend, was busy.

Chapter Thirteen

"I didn't see Hannah at church this morning," Charlotte said as she and Bob returned to the house. "I'm a bit worried."

"About what? You were just there yesterday when we brought Frank home. She seemed just fine then."

"That's the trouble. She seemed too fine." Charlotte tied on her apron and opened her refrigerator. She didn't have to worry about lunch for the rest of the family. Emily was still at camp, Christopher had gone home with his friend Dylan after church, and Sam was skateboarding.

Charlotte was thankful for that. It seemed since Arielle started at Jenny's Creamery all she heard from Sam was complaints about how they never spent any time together. She really liked Arielle and knew she was a steadying influence in Sam's life.

"I'm confused," Bob said, getting a glass of water. "How can she be too fine?"

"I don't know," Charlotte muttered, digging through her refrigerator, trying to find enough ingredients to put a healthy meal together for the Carters. Maybe roast chicken, she thought, since she had one defrosted. "I just get the feeling she's trying too hard."

"Well, you know Hannah. She's always such a rock."

"I think that's part of the problem," Charlotte said, thinking back to yesterday. When Charlotte and Bob drove Frank and Hannah home from the hospital, Charlotte had offered to stay awhile, but Hannah, seemingly back to her capable and in-charge self, had waved away Charlotte's offer. Nor had she taken Charlotte up on her proposal to get women from the church to bring meals for the two of them.

"I think you're trying to see problems where none exist," Bob grumbled. "If she doesn't want any help, you just have to accept that. Hannah is independent."

Charlotte acknowledged his comment with a nod and got to work on her chicken. She couldn't shake the feeling that something else was going on.

While she and Bob had sandwiches for lunch, the chicken cooked. As soon as it was done, Charlotte put it in a box along with a sugar-free cake she had baked and carried everything out to the car.

When she got to Hannah's place her resolve faltered a little. As Bob said, Hannah was an independent sort. Nonetheless, Charlotte wanted to help her friend. She strode up the walk and knocked on the door before she could change her mind.

"Charlotte, this is a surprise," Hannah said as she opened the door. "Come in. Come in."

"I brought you dinner," Charlotte said, handing Hannah the box. "Thought you could use a break."

Hannah frowned as if she couldn't understand what her friend was saying. "I don't need a break. Frank is home. Everything is fine." She gave Charlotte a bright smile. "But thanks for thinking of us." She took the box and set it on the counter, but Charlotte caught the scent of a roast cooking in the oven and noticed an array of muffins on the counter.

Hannah had been busy herself.

Frank was settled into his easy chair, the oxygen concentrator hissing beside him. Charlotte was encouraged by the color in his cheeks and the brightness of his eyes.

"Frank, you're looking good."

"He is, isn't he?" Hannah said, fussing with a blanket over Frank's knees.

"I'm so glad to be home." Frank caught Hannah's hand. "My wife has been such a support to me. I don't know what I would do without her."

Hannah glanced down at Frank and patted his hand. "And I don't know what I would do without you."

"Nice of you to stop by," Frank said. "How is everything at home?"

Charlotte sat down across from him, watching Hannah as she flitted about the room, adjusting the air conditioning, tidying, and doing busywork that niggled at Charlotte.

"I brought you some supper, but I'm guessing you won't need it."

Frank laughed. "No. Hannah's been cooking up a storm. Trying to find just the right recipe that will work with the new diet I have to follow."

"Not as easy as it looks," Hannah harrumphed. "I've been through about six different muffin recipes to find one that has enough fiber, not too much fat, and still retains some flavor." She shot Charlotte an exasperated glance. "It's a challenge; I can tell you that."

"Did you sleep well?" Charlotte asked Frank, slipping into daily chitchat and wishing her friend would sit down.

"Like a log. Good to be back in my own bed, though for a bit I thought I'd never be back here."

"Don't say that," Hannah snapped. "That's just crazy talk."

"It's the truth," Frank said with a shrug. "I'm just thankful the Lord saw fit to keep me on this earth awhile longer."

"You're going to get better enough to take that trip we always talked about," Hannah said.

Frank just smiled.

"You don't need to stay, you know," Hannah said. "I know you're tired yourself."

Charlotte took the hint and got up. "Okay. I just thought I would see how you all are doing."

"You don't worry about us at all," Hannah said with a dismissive flap of her hands. "You need to get back to your family."

"Are you sure you don't want me to set up a schedule for people to bring you meals for a while?" Charlotte asked.

"Don't be silly," Hannah said, straightening a cloth on her coffee table. "Frank and I can manage just fine." She glanced around the room, looking everywhere, it seemed, but at Charlotte or Frank. "Everything is just fine."

"Getting help would make things easier for you."

Hannah finally looked at Charlotte, frowning. "There's no need for that. I'm taking good care of my husband."

The note of finality in her voice gave Charlotte pause.

"Okay."

"Besides, if I need any help, I can ask."

That was true enough. Charlotte had to trust that her friend knew her own limits. She wished she knew, however, why Hannah was so adamant about doing everything herself.

"ARE YOU SURE this thing will start?" Aunt Dana stood with her hands on her hips, staring at the old truck they had cleared the grass away from.

When Aunt Dana had told him she couldn't help him until Monday, Christopher thought the day would never come. Now it was here, and finally he and Aunt Dana could work on the float. After all, the Fourth of July parade was in less than two weeks.

"Yes. I'm sure."

"How do you know?"

Christopher shrugged, a feeling of guilt washing over him. "Before you came I tried to start it."

"That was kind of dangerous, Christopher," Aunt Dana said, frowning. "You should have waited for me."

Seemed like all he was doing lately was waiting. But now they could get to work.

"It won't explode or anything like that," Christopher said, feeling frustrated.

Everyone always treated him like a little kid. And they never let him forget the time he and his friend Dylan had an accident with the tractor. "I bet I could drive it."

Aunt Dana looked past him to the shed, where Uncle Pete was working. "I wonder if we could get Pete to help us."

"I already asked," Christopher said with a sigh. "He and Grandpa are busy."

"I guess if it'll start, we can move it around ourselves." Aunt Dana walked around the truck, looking it over. "We can staple material or fringes to the bed to hide the wheels, put some fencing around the back."

"Oh! Oh! I know!" Christopher gave a little hop of excitement. "We could put that old shed on it. We could do, like, a pioneer scene. We've got the old grain grinder and the old flail. We can use those. And maybe the plow."

Aunt Dana frowned. "The truck bed is awfully small for all of that."

"But if we push things together," Christopher continued.

"Sorry, honey. There's just not enough room."

Christopher tried not to be disappointed. He had such great ideas, and every time he wanted to do one, something got in the way.

"Could we use the big hay wagon and pull it with the tractor? That would be plenty big enough," Aunt Dana suggested.

Christopher sighed again. "I asked Grandpa, but he said no." Seemed like that was all he ever heard around here. No. No. No.

"Okay. Well, we've got this truck. It's a start."

"I have such good ideas," Christopher said. "But we can't do any of them."

"Tell me anyway." She sat down beside him, looking at him like she really wanted to know. "What else were you thinking?"

"Well, I was thinking we could do a big farm scene showing how they used to make bread. We could start at one end of the float with a sack of seed and that old plow, and that seed-spreader thingy. Then we could show the flail and that old wheat grinder, and after that a couple of loaves of bread. Maybe Grandma could bake them. I even asked Sam if he wanted to be a farmer on the float, but he just looked at me like I had three heads when I asked. I know he just wants to look cool in front of Arielle and in front of his friends so he won't do it."

Aunt Dana sighed. "Sam is a little overly concerned about his image."

Christopher didn't want to talk about Sam and whatever image Aunt Dana was talking about. All he knew was that lately Sam had been snappy and grumpy.

"You have some really, really good ideas, Christopher," Aunt Dana said. "Too bad we don't have something bigger to put everything on."

"What could we do instead?" Christopher asked, looking over the stuff they had pulled out of the shed.

Aunt Dana tapped her chin, pursing her lips. "We'll think of something. For now, let's make sure this truck works."

"It's kind of low on gas," Christopher said.

"Then we'll fill it up. Where are the gas tanks?"

How could she miss them? The two large tanks were still shiny with the new paint job the television people had given them last summer when they filmed the music video at the farm.

"Wait, I see them," Aunt Dana said. She got into the truck, and Christopher scrambled up inside as well.

"It's a standard, you know," Christopher said. "You'll have to pump the gas if it doesn't start right away."

"How do you know so much about trucks?" Aunt Dana gave him a funny look, like she was surprised. "You have all kinds of smarts, don't you?"

"I listen to Uncle Pete and Grandpa talk. And Uncle Pete's truck, Lazarus, is kind of funny and needs to be helped along. At least that's what he always says." Christopher grinned back at Aunt Dana, feeling proud that she thought he was smart.

"I know all too well how much help old Lazarus needs." Aunt Dana laughed. "Okay, let's go." She let out the clutch, and the truck jumped ahead and then stalled.

"That was close," Aunt Dana said with a grin. She pumped the gas and turned the key again. The engine rolled over and over and over, sounding like it was complaining, and then finally the engine fired up. This time she was more careful when she let out the clutch. The truck lurched forward again but then slowed to a crawl. They got to the gas tanks.

Christopher was just about to get out when he saw the horses standing by the fence.

"I'm going to make sure the gate to the horse pasture is closed," he said, not wanting to take any chances.

"Which gas do I use?" Aunt Dana called out as Christopher ran toward the gate.

"The one that says gas," Christopher called out.

Thankfully the gate was closed properly and the horses were just being curious. Christopher petted Shania and Ben and then walked back to the truck.

Aunt Dana had the nozzle in the gas tank of the truck and was already squeezing the handle. "How much should I put in?" she asked.

"Listen real careful. When you hear it start to gurgle in the tank, then you know you have enough." Christopher bent over and petted Toby, who was jumping around him.

"Do you think we should throw candies off the float?" he asked.

"Maybe we could throw pieces of bread," Aunt Dana said with a laugh.

Christopher laughed too. "I don't think that would work very well. Maybe we could throw out granola bars."

"Maybe. We'll have to see if we can find some small ones." Aunt Dana was quiet for a moment. "I think the tank is full," she said, taking the nozzle out.

"You have to hang it up where it was when you're done," Christopher said, bending over to pet Toby.

"Hey, guys, what's up?" Uncle Pete called out, coming out from the tractor shed. He was wiping his hands on a greasy cloth, his coveralls full of dirt. He frowned at the truck parked by the gas tanks. "You actually got that old thing to run?"

"Christopher started it this morning," Aunt Dana said, sounding proud of him.

Uncle Pete looked surprised. "Christopher started it, eh? Can't believe it's still running. The O-rings must be petrified by now."

"We just gassed it up, and now we're moving it closer to the shed."

Uncle Pete lifted one eyebrow. "What in the world are you going to do with it?"

"We're making a float for the Fourth of July parade," Christopher said. "Like I told you."

"On that old truck? It's not big enough, is it?"

"It's the only thing I could find to use," Christopher answered.

Uncle Pete glanced at Dana. "And you're helping?"
"Trying to."
"Let's see if it gets going," Christopher said, jumping into the truck. Uncle Pete was about to get in the driver's side when Aunt Dana stopped him. "I gassed it up—I'll drive."

Uncle Pete held his hands up. "Of course." Then he walked around the truck and got in. Christopher had to scooch over to the middle, but he didn't mind.

Aunt Dana got in, turned the key, and the engine roared to life.

"Yay! This will work great," Christopher said, grinning at Aunt Dana.

She put it in gear, turned it around, and drove it slowly toward the house. As they got closer, the porch door opened and Grandpa stepped outside. He was still holding his newspaper, and his glasses were pushed up on his forehead.

"I think we woke Dad up from his nap," Uncle Pete said with a grin.

Then the truck started running slower and slower. Aunt Dana pumped the gas, but nothing helped.

"You sure you put enough gas in?" Uncle Pete leaned forward to ask Dana.

"I'm sure. I filled it until I heard gurgling, like Christopher told me." Aunt Dana said.

Then the truck quit completely.

Uncle Pete got out and lifted the hood just as Grandpa came closer. Christopher's good mood slipped away again. Nothing was going right. He got out of the truck, hoping

Uncle Pete or Grandpa would know what was wrong with the truck.

Uncle Pete was pulling on something, tugging on something else.

"What tank did you use to fill it up?" Uncle Pete was asking.

"The one by the barn."

"There're two tanks there," Grandpa said.

"I think I used the one closest to the house."

"There's your problem," Uncle Pete said. "You put gas in a diesel engine. Recipe for disaster; the engine is well and truly cooked now."

"Cooked? Does that mean it won't go anymore?" Christopher had hung around Uncle Pete and Grandpa enough to know what they meant when they said stuff like that.

"'Fraid not." Uncle Pete shook his head. "Ruined this truck completely. Won't be worth spending any time on."

Christopher leaned back against the truck. Of course this would happen. Sure, the truck wasn't big enough for what he needed, but at least it was something to build the float on.

Chapter Fourteen

As Charlotte turned onto the road leading to the farm, she mentally went over her grocery checklist. She was pretty sure she'd gotten everything, but at the same time no matter how careful she was, it seemed she always forgot something.

Then, as she made the turn into the driveway, she realized what it was.

Christopher had specifically asked her to get a new kind of cereal he'd seen on television. He'd been asking for the past three weeks and she kept forgetting.

Now she'd forgotten again.

She sighed, guilt eating at her yet again. She would just have to explain to him that sometimes older people forget things. Trouble was, when it came to the things Christopher wanted and needed, she felt as if she were failing him.

She still hadn't patched his pants.

As she turned into the yard, more guilt dogging her, she saw an old flatbed farm truck parked in front of the house, hood up, Bob and Pete peering into the depths of the engine.

Dana stood to one side, biting her lip. Christopher sat on the ground, staring sightlessly ahead.

What was going on?

Charlotte got out of the car and walked toward the gathering. "What's happening? And what is this truck doing here?" she asked.

"Nothing, it seems." Bob pulled away from the vehicle, wiping the grease on his hands with his handkerchief. "This truck is toast."

"How did it get here?" Charlotte looked past Pete, who was still bent over the engine, to Dana, who hovered beside him, looking stricken.

"Christopher started it up." Pete pulled away and slammed the hood shut. The sound reverberated through the quiet of the yard. "But it's wrecked."

"How did that happen?"

Bob glanced at Dana, who was now looking down at her dusty running shoes. A smear of grease marred her white jeans, and her shirt was liberally coated with dust.

What had she been doing?

"I...uh...put the wrong gas in the truck."

Charlotte frowned, still not sure why the old truck was running in the first place, but no one seemed to be cluing her in.

She looked at Christopher. "Why did you want to get this truck going? It's been parked for years."

"And now it's going to be parked forever," Pete added.

"I wanted something for a float," Christopher blurted out, jumping to his feet. "And I couldn't use anything else. And no one wanted to help me except Aunt Dana. And I found the truck, and I started it up. And Aunt Dana said she would put gas in it, but I didn't watch her because I had to check the horses. I didn't want Uncle Pete to get mad at me if they got out again because I forgot to close the gate. And I forgot to tell Aunt Dana which gas tank to use. And then she put the wrong gas in, and I didn't know it was a diesel truck." Christopher's voice rose with every *and*. "And now everyone is mad, and I don't have a truck or anything to put my float on."

Christopher dashed a hand over his eyes and then spun around and ran across the yard toward the barn, Toby on his heels.

"What's gotten into him?" Pete grumbled.

A moment of silence followed Pete's question, and then Dana spoke up.

"I think he feels like no one cares about his projects," Dana said quietly. "Maybe he's feeling a little ignored."

Pete gave a laugh. "Of course we care about him. I got mad at him because he should have secured the gates after the two of you checked the horses."

"*I* should have secured the gates," Dana said quietly. "It was *my* fault, and you should have gotten angry with me that the horses got out." She pushed her hair away from her face with a sigh. "I think he's just feeling like a youngest child right now. Ignored and unappreciated."

Another stone of guilt dropped onto Charlotte's shoulders. She should have seen this coming. She too had expected a lot of Christopher. "I know I've been at fault too," she said quietly. "I've asked him to take on some of Emily's chores because I was so busy trying to help Hannah."

Bob sighed and crossed his arms over his chest, looking in the direction Christopher had gone. "He asked me to help him with a float for the Fourth of July parade, and I said I didn't have time. Then he asked if he could use the farm truck or the hay wagon, and I said he couldn't." Bob glanced at Charlotte and gave her a wry smile. "I feel kind of bad. Especially after hearing Frank talk about regrets. I guess I don't want to be talking the same way someday."

"I'm sure he would love it if you could help him," Charlotte said. "Maybe I should help too."

"I suppose I can spare some time," Pete offered.

"You've got to work on the haybine," Bob said.

"It's almost done."

"Well, when it's completely done then you can help," Bob said. Then he walked across the yard toward the barn.

"Now I'm starting to understand how Christopher feels," Pete said. But he was grinning.

Charlotte had to smile. "I'm sure there have been times when you've felt the same way."

"Yeah." Pete pushed his hat back on his head and blew out his breath. "I just feel bad that I didn't recognize how he was feeling. I shouldn't have yelled at him about the horses."

"And I shouldn't have expected him to cover for Emily, Sam, and me while I was gone," Charlotte added. She glanced at Dana. "At least you've been helping him."

Dana shrugged. "I haven't done much. Seems everything I've tried to do to help around here has backfired." Then she brightened. "But if we can use the hay wagon, then we can do just what Christopher wanted to do all along." She tapped Pete on the shoulder. "And I've got just the job for you, mister."

"I knew I should be afraid of that look in your eye," Pete said with a sigh. "For now, you can help me haul this truck back to the barn."

Charlotte watched them walk off together toward the tractor and smiled. Another crisis averted. But on the heels of that came thoughts of Hannah. She wished she could feel better about Hannah taking on the bulk of Frank's care.

She also wished Hannah would open up to her; she was fairly sure her dear friend was holding something back.

"ARE WE GETTING to the end of the trail?" Ashley grumbled. "Riding this horse is like sitting on a barrel."

Emily glanced over her shoulder at her friend, leaning over her saddle. The sun, broken by the leaves overhead, danced over her red hair and shone off her red face. "At least it's cooler riding than it would be playing volleyball on the beach."

Ashley kicked her horse and came alongside Emily, grunting with each thud of her horse's hooves. "Remind me again why this was a better idea."

"Nicole. Mike. They both signed up for the volleyball tournament after we did."

Ashley sighed. "You can't avoid both of them forever."

"I know. I just don't trust Nicole and I don't want her to see me with Mike."

"I don't think Mike's a stalker, you know."

Emily sighed as she nudged her horse to step over a large log. "I know. But I think Nicole might be. I wish I could figure her out."

"What's to figure out?" Ashley released a snort that made Emily's horse jump to the side. Emily settled it down, and they fell back into a steady, plodding rhythm that could have put Emily to sleep if she'd been on one of her own horses.

"What do you mean?"

"She's jealous," Ashley said. "She's always been jealous of you."

"Jealous?" Emily frowned. "Of what?"

Ashley gave Emily a wry look. "C'mon. You're dating Troy, and on top of that you snagged the attention of the cutest guy at camp."

"He's a friend."

"I know, but the time you spent with him meant Nicole couldn't make a move on him."

"Well, she can make a move on him now."

"He doesn't want her to."

Emily felt confused. "I thought camp was about making your relationship with Jesus better. Not about flirting and all that."

"It happens, and with Nicole it seems to happen often."

"It's just frustrating," Emily said. "I feel like all the good stuff I'm learning about how to be a better person, how to let Jesus make me a better person, is worn away each time I see Nicole. And she's the daughter of the minister. You'd think she'd be the best example of how to be a good Christian."

"I sometimes think because she's the minister's daughter she figures she's got the most to prove—that she's cool after all and not a goody-goody."

Emily laughed. "Who uses those words anymore?"

"I do," Ashley said with a groan. "When my behind is so sore I can't think of anything else to say."

"Well, your poor behind is about to get a break. I see the end of the trail."

They broke out into the open, and the horses ahead of them started to trot.

"Oh, great!" Ashley said. "As if I don't hurt enough."

"Keep pressure on the reins if you don't want to trot," Emily said.

But Ashley either didn't care or couldn't do what Emily suggested, and her horse started trotting, making her hair bounce with each step.

Emily held her horse back. Uncle Pete had always said it was important to make your horse do what *you* wanted, not what *it* wanted. A few horses passed her, their riders hanging onto the pommel of the saddle, reins flopping.

By the time Emily got to the paddock, most of the other riders were dismounting, groaning and complaining.

Emily didn't know what their problem was. She'd had fun.

"Tie up your horses," Adam, their leader, instructed them as he dismounted from his horse. "All saddles are to be brought here to the barn, and don't forget to brush your horses when you're done."

Emily dismounted, loosened the cinch, and pulled the saddle and blanket off, grunting from the weight. The smell of hot horse assailed her nostrils, but it was a good smell. It reminded her of home.

For a moment, she missed the farm. Just a little.

She set the saddle on the ground and pulled the cinch up and hooked it over the horn so it wouldn't flop while she walked.

"So, have fun?"

Emily bit her lip, closed her eyes, and sent up a quick prayer for patience. Then she turned to Nicole.

"Yeah. I did."

"Missed you at the tournament," Nicole said. "I think Mike missed you too."

Emily picked up the saddle and trudged over to the tack shed, preferring to ignore Nicole.

Emily handed Adam the saddle, took a curry brush from the tack shed, and returned to her horse, still tied to the hitching post. Nicole was standing next to it, stroking its nose.

Emily sighed. "What do you want, Nicole?"

Nicole just shrugged and then pulled something out of her pocket, giving Emily just a glimpse of her cell phone before she put it back in her pocket. "The reception here is just great. I've been able to text all week. Keep the people back home up to date on what's been happening here."

Emily's heart jumped into her throat. "What are you trying to tell me?"

Nicole just shrugged. "Shall I say hi to Troy for you? Give him your love?"

With a feeling of dread, Emily realized exactly what Nicole meant.

"You wouldn't," she said.

Nicole shrugged. "Maybe. Maybe not." Then with a waggle of her fingers, she strutted away, looking as if she were on top of the world.

Emily brushed her horse, her mind going a mile a minute. What if Nicole actually called Troy? What would she tell him? What kind of spin would she put on what she saw?

Whatever she wants, Emily realized.

She knew one thing. She had to contact Troy herself before Nicole did.

She quickly finished brushing her horse and led it into the corral.

"So that's done," Ashley said, walking stiff-legged toward her friend. "What shall we do until suppertime?"

Emily glanced at Ashley. "I gotta run."

"But..."

Emily took off for the cabin. She burst through the door and opened her locker. She dug out the money Mrs. Carter had given her and then ran to the telephone.

She stopped in her tracks. The line was fifteen people long. Soon the bell would ring for suppertime, and the phone would be off limits until tomorrow at noon.

And that might be too late.

Chapter Fifteen

"Are you sure you can fix it?" Lena hovered over the photocopier while Sam knelt down in front of it on Wednesday afternoon. He wasn't sure himself, but he'd learned a thing or two from helping Uncle Pete and Grandpa fix equipment.

"I think we can take this panel off." Sam pressed a recessed latch, and sure enough, off it came. He set it aside and then pulled off another panel and peered in. "Here's the problem." He reached in and carefully tugged out two crumpled-up papers. "It was just jammed."

"Bless you, boy," Lena said with a heavy sigh. "You just saved me from having to call the technician. Again."

"It's not a big deal." Sam couldn't believe no one could figure out how to unjam the copier. "It's not that hard." He snapped the panels back in place and pressed the power button. The copier whirred to life and then spat out the copies Lena had been waiting for.

"Amazing. I think we'll keep you around, mister," she said with a grin. "Now you make sure you don't stay so long tonight. You're too young to be hanging around the office after hours."

"I just wanted to make sure I got everything done."

She smiled at him. "You're a capable worker, Sam." Then she patted him on the shoulder and walked back to her desk.

Sam walked back to the file room, feeling pretty good about himself. He hadn't made any major mistakes today. Even Mrs. Pictou couldn't find fault with his work—a small miracle in itself. He glanced around the orderly file room with a feeling of satisfaction. He stopped by the coffee room to make sure everything was ready in case Uncle Bill or his partner still wanted another cup of coffee.

Check and double-check.

He tugged off his tie as he headed toward his car, whistling a tune. Things were looking up. Even better, he and Arielle were finally going out tonight.

He got in his car and waited until he was out of River Bend before he called her on his cell phone.

"Hey, what's up?" he asked when she answered. "We still on for tonight?"

"Tonight?"

"Yeah. We talked about it the other day, remember?"

Her pause wasn't encouraging. "I thought it was up in the air."

"*I* thought you said we'd go if you didn't have to work." Sam felt a beat of frustration. "Are you working tonight?"

"No. I'm not."

"So what should we do?" He tapped his fingers on the steering wheel.

His question was followed by another pause, which only increased his uneasiness.

"Well, here's the thing. I . . . uh . . . made other plans."

Sam frowned. "With who?"

"Some friends."

Sam tried not to squeeze his cell phone too tight. "We haven't seen each other for a while."

"You don't need to snap at me."

Sam pressed his lips together, counted to three, and took a breath. "I'm sorry. I thought that if you weren't working, then ipso facto, we'd be going out." He took a breath to calm himself. "That's a legal term I picked up hanging around the lawyers at the office," he said in a lame attempt at a joke.

Her feeble chuckle told him how flat his joke had landed.

"I wasn't sure how serious you were," she said. "I thought it was just a maybe. You know?"

"No. I don't know." Though he had tried to hold his anger back he couldn't keep the bitterness out of his voice. "Ever since you started working at Jenny's, I've been trying to find time to go out with you. You're either tired, or working, or you're sick or something." He glanced down at the speedometer and eased his foot off the gas. A speeding ticket from Arielle's father would put the icing on the cake right now. "I've been pretty serious about trying to go out with my own girlfriend."

Arielle's sigh gave him a lurch of dread.

"We need to talk about that, Sam."

"About what?"

"About this boyfriend-girlfriend thing," she said.

Sam frowned and eased his foot off the accelerator again. "Explain what you mean."

"Well . . . you're going to be attending one college, and I'm going to a different college, and we won't be seeing much of each other once that happens." She gave a light sigh. "So I'm just wondering how that would work for us."

Sam was speeding again. He slowed down, spied a side road, and pulled onto it. Then he stopped the car. "I think it would mean we phone each other, e-mail, text, Skype, chat, Facebook. There's all kinds of ways to keep in touch."

"I'm not sure that's what I want."

"What *do* you want, Arielle? Why don't you just tell me, and we'll see what we can do about it?"

Sam leaned his head back against the headrest of his car. He shoved his hand through his hair, wishing he could think of something to say to change the direction of this conversation. Because, right now, he had a bad feeling about where it was headed.

"I think . . . I think I want us to break up."

He let out a pent-up breath. He was right. He *didn't* like this at all.

"You *think* you want us to break up?"

"I guess . . . I know."

Sam closed his eyes and counted to ten. Then again.

"Sam?"

"Yeah, I'm still here." He released a bitter laugh. "And I can't believe you want to break up with me over the phone."

The car was suddenly too small. He shoved the door open and jumped out, needing to be outside where there was space for what was happening.

"Well, it's been hard to see each other."

"And whose fault is that?" Sam walked away from his car, trying to keep his anger under control. "You can't put that on my shoulders."

"I know, Sam. I guess, I just knew for a while now..."

"Why did you get back together with me, if you were going to break up with me anyway?"

"I'm sorry, Sam." He heard a sniff on the other end. Great. Now Arielle was crying. "I have to go. Please don't come to see me."

"Why not? Don't you want to talk about this?"

"There's nothing to talk about, Sam. I won't...I can't change my mind. I'm sorry."

And then she hung up.

Sam held the phone to his ear a moment longer, disbelief coursing through him. One small part of him still hoped she would click through again and say it was all a mistake.

But nothing.

He closed his phone and shook his head. He still couldn't believe it. He tried to call her home number again.

And got the answering machine.

Sam slapped the phone shut, striding back and forth in front of his car. She had just broken up with him over the phone. Like he wasn't even important enough to talk to face-to-face.

He stopped, glared at his phone, and then swung his hand back and pitched the phone through the air.

Then he dove into his car, slapped the gearshift into drive, and spun out onto the road.

He didn't know where he was going, and it didn't matter. No way he was going back to the farm or any place in Bedford.

Dark sky lay ahead of him. Behind him the sun eased below the horizon. Still early evening. Now what?

Sam drove past the road leading home. And then drove on. Half an hour later, without any conscious decision on his part, he found himself heading down the road along the lake. Heading toward the Vances' cabin.

A few minutes later, he turned down the driveway to the cabin and was greeted by a blaze of light. Every room in the cabin was lit up.

As he got out of the car, he heard music thumping out of speakers set out on the deck. Laughter drifted back to him from the lake as did the snap and crackle of a fire on the beach.

He stood by his car a moment, second thoughts chasing his anger through his mind.

He should just go home. This was not where he belonged.

Then, just as he was about to get back into his car to drive away, a female voice squealed out his name.

"Hey, Sam! Good to see you." Sarah, a girl he had met the last time he was here, ran down the steps of the house straight to him. The words on her T-shirt, BORN TO PARTY, glittered in the glow of light from the house. Her long, black hair hung loose to her waist.

"I was hoping you'd show." She grinned, her dark eyes glinting up at him. "You coming to the beach?" Sarah asked him, giving his arm a tug. "We've got a fire going. I can roast you a hot dog."

Sam's stomach rumbled, reminding him he hadn't eaten anything since breakfast. "I could have something to eat."

"We've got pizza too if you don't like hot dogs. And chips and pop and cookies." She giggled. "I made them."

"In that case..." Sam let Sarah pull him toward the fire. He would stay only a while, he told himself. Just a while.

"You just sit down. I'll get a hot dog bun ready for you," Sarah said.

"Sit over here, Sam," Artie called out, moving aside. With a grin, Sam sat down on an empty stump by the fire.

Wilson slipped a cold can in his hand. "You look thirsty," he said. "Drink up." Wilson dropped onto a lawn chair beside him. "Glad you came. I was hoping you'd get here." He tipped his can toward Sarah, who stood by the picnic table fixing Sam's hot dog. "Sarah was *really* hoping you'd come."

Sam glanced toward where she stood. Sarah flashed him a smile that made him feel a bit better.

He looked away, taking a quick sip of the pop.

Only it wasn't pop. It was beer.

Wilson elbowed him. "Pretty good stuff, eh?"

Sam glanced from his friend to the can sprinkled with condensation. Then he thought, why not? He hadn't had the best of days.

Besides, he was among people who liked him. He was going to eat something. Finish this can of beer. Have a bit of fun with his new friends. What was the harm in that?

"SO, AS WE GET READY to sing the last song of the evening, I just want all of you to remember that God listens and that He cares."

The worship leader, Colette, looked around the auditorium, and for a moment Emily felt as if she were talking specifically to her.

The week and a half had been a mix of fun, challenges, and things she'd never heard before. She'd seen people cry, laugh, sing, and pray. She'd experienced community and adventure.

It had been fun and interesting.

"And now, our worship team will lead us in the song we've spent the last few days learning. I want to hear all of you sing it with your voice and with your heart." Colette put the microphone in the mic stand and then walked away as Mike and his group took over.

"Okay. You heard her. Let's sing!" Mike yelled into the microphone.

The first chords of the song blasted out of the speakers. Emily jumped, but then as the band started singing the now-familiar words, she sang along, clapping along with everyone else.

A feeling unlike anything else she'd ever experienced flowed through her as she sang; suddenly she knew for sure that God was real and that He cared about her.

She glanced at Ashley, who was wiping tears from her eyes, and she realized Ashley felt the same.

When the last chord of the song sounded, Emily gave in to an urge and hugged her friend with one arm. "That song is so good," she whispered in Ashley's ear.

Ashley grinned back at Emily and returned the hug with enthusiasm.

In that moment, Emily sensed she and Ashley had connected on another level. It felt like their friendship had deepened and flourished.

They stood together for a moment longer, and then the movement of the people around them made them pull apart. People were dispersing, and the chatter around them was rising up. Their fellow campers were ready to move on to the next thing.

"Are you going to campfire?" Ashley asked, slipping on her jacket.

"I think so."

Ashley glanced from Emily to Mike, who was kneeling down on the stage, putting his guitar away. "I should let you know, Nicole's been talking about you two again," Ashley said, leaning closer to Emily and lowering her voice.

"I guessed as much." Emily wondered if Nicole had followed through on her veiled threat to phone Troy.

"Like I told you, she's just jealous."

"Maybe." Then guilt grabbed at Emily. "I guess I shouldn't judge her, should I?"

Ashley squeezed Emily's arm. "You're such a cool friend. I'm proud to know you."

They made it outside, and the group split up. The younger campers went back to their cabins, and the older ones drifted over to the campfire.

Emily settled down on what she now considered *her* stump, thankful for the cooling breeze coming off the lake. The evening was still warm, and sitting in the auditorium for an hour had been a bit stifling.

"What are all of you going to do when you get back to the real world?" one of the counselors asked the group. "Let's hear your plans—and I want you to use the word *two* in your answers."

"Take a two-hour bath," someone called out.

"Watch television for two days."

"Sleep for two weeks."

Emily laughed; the thought made her yawn. Ashley elbowed her. "Looks like you'll be doing that too," she said.

"I didn't think I could get by with only four hours of sleep," Emily said, yawning again.

"The way you've been avoiding me, I thought you'd be getting way more sleep than that."

Mike dropped into the sand on the other side of Emily, wrapping his arms around his knees.

Emily glanced down at him, and her cheeks flushed. "Not really avoiding you. Just..." She hesitated, not sure what to say.

"Just not sure your boyfriend at home would approve?"

The burden on Emily's heart shifted. "I guess."

"Hey, I know how it goes. But we're friends, right?" His smile made her feel good.

"Right. Friends." She grinned. Then she yawned again, her jaw almost cracking. "Oh, boy. I really have to get to bed on time tonight."

Ashley laughed out loud.

"On the last night of camp?" Ashley's tone was mocking. "No one goes to bed at all on the last night of camp, girl."

"If you try to sleep, I'm sure someone will make sure you don't," Mike added.

"You're kidding, right?"

Ashley and Mike just laughed again. Which gave Emily her answer. *Not.*

The leader called out another question, and another round of answers followed.

The conversation grew lower, quieter as the evening wore on; in spite of being interested in what people were saying, Emily's eyes grew heavier and heavier.

"Hey. You can't go to sleep." Mike elbowed her and handed her a can of pop. "Slug this down. It will get you going again."

Emily took the chilled can and got to her feet. "I think I need to go for a walk."

"Don't even think about heading back to the cabin," Ashley warned.

"I'll chaperone her." Mike got to his feet. Emily's heart lifted at the thought of being alone with Mike once again even though she still worried others might get the wrong impression.

She cracked open her pop and took a couple of sips, the cold drink waking her up.

Silently, she and Mike headed back to the dock, the first place they had bonded.

They were quiet as they walked over the wooden planks, the light of the moon illuminating the way. It was a perfect night, Emily thought, shoving her free hand into the pocket of her oversize sweater.

She looked at the light of the moon glimmering over the water and wished Troy were here. The thought of him gave her a chill. What if Nicole had called him? What if Nicole was watching her even now?

She glanced over her shoulder, shivering although the air was warm. What was she doing here with Mike?

Spending time with a friend, she reminded herself.

"Tomorrow we go back," Mike said, his voice quiet in the soft darkness.

"Yeah. I'm looking forward to seeing my family again." Emily smiled, thinking of the letter she'd received yesterday from Christopher telling her how much he missed having her around. "I've never been away from them this long before." She sat down on the dock, looking out over the lake.

"You're pretty lucky to have family," Mike said.

"I guess I am." Emily usually thought of her family as people who were just always there. "Are you looking forward to going home?"

Mike just shrugged, and Emily realized that for him, *home* meant a place without his mother.

She took another sip of pop and then touched his arm. "Like I told you before, it gets a little better. The sadness. It takes time and a bunch of tears, but it does ease off."

Mike gave a short laugh and then sighed. "I guess I can trust you. You would know."

"Yeah. I would." Emily took another sip of the pop. She swung her legs back and forth as the cool air brushed her face.

Mike sat down beside her, his elbows resting on his knees as he stared out over the water, saying nothing.

"I want to thank you again," Emily said after a moment of quiet.

Mike angled her a quick smile. "For what?"

"For rescuing me last week. I didn't get a chance to thank you properly."

"Yeah. I noticed you were kind of avoiding me."

"Well, this girl from home has been watching me; she's trying to make trouble between me and my boyfriend. I'm glad I had this chance to thank you for saving my life."

"Don't get dramatic." He turned away and released a short laugh. "I just pulled you out of the water. Nothing more."

Emily frowned at his curt reply. "Why are you angry?"

Mike didn't respond, and in the silence a startling revelation came to Emily. She put her hand on his arm and gently squeezed. "Are you thinking about your mom?"

Mike just stared ahead. Then he sighed. "Yeah. How did you know?"

"Good guess."

"She shouldn't have drowned. She shouldn't have. It's all my fault." His angry words were like a stain on the perfect night.

Emily frowned. "How do you figure that?"

Mike closed his eyes and shook his head back and forth. "I should have gone in the boat with her. I could have saved her."

"How can you possibly think it's your fault?"

"Maybe if I had been a bit faster, swam a bit harder..." His voice broke off, and to Emily's surprise she saw the glistening track of a tear on his cheek.

The sight melted her heart, and she slipped her arm over his shoulders. "That seems like a lot to put on yourself."

He didn't reply, but Emily saw the lines around his mouth soften. "It's hard not to. I keep replaying things in my mind."

Emily caught herself, remembering her own feelings

when her mother died. How she had blamed herself. Blamed other people.

"Well, you saved me. If you hadn't been there, I would have drowned the other day. You saved me, and I'm so thankful you did."

Mike drew a long breath and then turned to her. "You mean that?"

"I *know* it."

To her relief, he smiled. His eyes, dark and shining, held hers, and it seemed as if everything slowed down.

He touched her arm, and as if it were the most natural thing in the world, they leaned closer and then he kissed her on the cheek.

Emily jerked back at the same time Mike did.

"I'm sorry," he said. "I shouldn't have done that."

"No. It's okay..." But was it? Emily wasn't sure what to make of his kiss. And of her reaction to it.

"What are you two doing out here in the dark?"

Emily's heart stuttered in her chest as she recognized the voice behind them.

Of course it would be Nicole. And of course she would be the one to see what had just happened.

But Mike kept his hand on Emily's arm and glanced back. "We're saying good-bye," he said, his voice even and quiet. "And I don't think we need your commentary."

"That looked like a lot more than saying good-bye," Nicole snapped.

Mike shrugged and shot Emily a grin. It was as if he was telling her to play along. "That's because you don't know the situation." He turned, looking back at her. "Do you?"

Nicole looked down on them, her arms crossed over her chest. Even in the half-light Emily saw her tight lips, the glint of anger in her eyes.

"I know what I see," she shot back.

"No. You don't." Mike let go of Emily and got to his feet to face Nicole. He towered over her. "Emily has a boyfriend, and I have a girlfriend. We're just good friends who share a sadness I hope you never have to feel."

Relief flowed through Emily as she heard what Mike was saying. As he spoke, she knew he was right. The moment had been intense, but it had had a different feeling than what she had with Troy.

"Well . . . ," was all Nicole could muster. She spun around and stomped off the dock.

Emily started to get up, and Mike caught her by the arm, helping her to her feet. "Are you okay?" he asked.

"Yeah. I'm fine." She gave him a quick smile. "Thanks for that. Nicole is a . . . I don't know. She has never liked me very much. Not sure why."

"I am." Mike grinned, his teeth white in the dark. Emily was relieved to see him smiling again. "She's jealous."

Emily frowned. Ashley had said the same thing. "Why would she be?"

"Because you're fun. You're self-confident. You're a trendsetter."

"I am not."

"Did you see what she was wearing?"

Emily shrugged. "Not really."

"Exactly the same thing you are. Scarf. A dress over skinny jeans. Lace-up boots. She's missing the chunky sweater and the hair band though."

"Since when do you notice what a girl wears?"

"Trained well by my girlfriend." Mike grinned again. "I think she'd like your style as well."

"That's just a coincidence," Emily said, still unable to absorb the fact that Nicole was jealous of her.

"I think it's deliberate," Mike said with a grin, easing away any discomfort Emily might have felt at his kiss a few moments ago.

Emily still didn't want to believe him, but her mind skipped back to other times when Nicole had seemed a little too aware of what Emily was wearing. Could he be right?

She shrugged. "If she is, that seems a bit weird."

"Anyway, she looked mad. So we should probably get back before she has a chance to spread any rumors around."

Which made Emily think about Nicole's cell phone and her threat.

Please, Lord, she prayed, *don't let her have done anything. Please don't let her call Troy before I have a chance to talk to him myself.*

They walked away from the dock, the noise from the group around the fire growing with each step. It didn't sound like people would settle down for some time.

"Do people really stay up all night the last night of camp?" Emily asked, her previous sleepiness returning.

"Oh, yeah. And so will you because if you even try to go to your cabin, you might end up dunked in the lake."

Emily shuddered. "I don't want to go in there again."

Mike laughed. "I'll protect you."

Emily laughed as well as they rejoined the group around

the fire and soon were drawn into a midnight scavenger hunt.

Emily and Mike were separated in the melee, and that was okay with her.

Though as the night wore on, the memory of his kiss hovered on the edges of her consciousness. She wasn't sure what to do with it.

Chapter Sixteen

"It's time for bed, young man," Charlotte said to Christopher as she entered the family room.

Her grandson looked up from the plans he and Bob were working on. "Can't I stay up just a little longer? It's summertime."

"It's already an hour and a half past your normal bedtime." Charlotte walked over to the table and looked over her husband's shoulder.

Bob, Christopher, and Dana had been working nonstop on the float since Monday.

Tonight Bob and Christopher had spent most of the evening trying to decide how they would arrange the various items Christopher had found.

Bob turned and looked up at Charlotte. "Has Sam called yet?"

Charlotte pressed her lips together, glanced at Christopher, and gave a slight shake of her head.

When Sam didn't come home for supper, she had tried to call his cell phone, thinking he might have stayed late at work. But he wasn't answering. She had called Bill at home, but he had told her that Sam left the office at five thirty. By seven Charlotte was growing more concerned and called Arielle. But Arielle wasn't home either. It was now nine thirty, and still no word from Sam.

Though she struggled not to worry, she had grown more and more apprehensive with each tick of the clock. Where could Sam be?

Her mind cycled back to another night, many years ago. The night when she and Bob had discovered a note from their daughter Denise, Sam's mother, telling them that she and her boyfriend had run away to get married.

Sam had finally settled down and had his own plans. He wouldn't do that, would he? And Arielle? Surely she was more responsible than that?

She brushed the worrying thoughts aside. There had to be a good reason for Sam's tardiness.

Bob, seeming to read the worry on her face, covered her hand with his and squeezed. "I'm sure everything is fine. Maybe his phone is dead."

Charlotte forced herself to smile at him and then turned back to the plans Christopher was working on. "Do you think you can get it ready in time for the parade?"

She had to focus on something else. Anything to keep her mind from imagining her grandson either eloping with his girlfriend or lying somewhere injured.

Christopher looked up at his grandfather. "We can, can't we?"

"Of course."

"For now, you'll have to leave your work until tomorrow. Go wash up, and I'll be up to tuck you in."

Christopher scampered off to the bathroom and

Charlotte watched him go, feeling suddenly melancholy when she saw the flash of his ankles beneath his pant legs. "He's growing up way too fast," she murmured to Bob. "I just bought him new pants, and they're already too short." A couple pairs of his other pants still needed patching.

Bob slowly pushed himself to his feet and stretched his arms above his head. His gusty sigh echoed Charlotte's own mood. "Seems like only a couple of days ago, he and the older kids came here," he said. "Now he's already twelve and full of plans."

"I'm glad you decided to help him with the float. What made you change your mind?"

Bob ran his hand over his thinning hair and gave a quick shrug. "I keep thinking about what Frank said, about having regrets. Made me realize maybe I didn't spend enough time with our kids while they were growing up. Now maybe I get a second chance with Sam, Emily, and Christopher."

"Frank's comment seemed sad," Charlotte said.

"Especially since he and Hannah don't have kids of their own." He glanced up at Charlotte. "How is Frank doing?"

Charlotte sighed. "I tried to call Hannah yesterday, but she didn't answer the phone. I was going to visit her today, but I've been so busy just trying to catch up here I didn't make it. The kids do keep us hopping."

"That they do." Bob picked up the pencils and folded up the float plans. "I guess I need to see that as a blessing. Take advantage of the time God has given us with them."

Charlotte slipped her arms around Bob and gave him a quick hug. "You're a good man," she said.

Bob patted her back and nodded. It might not be the most romantic gesture, but Charlotte knew Bob well enough to realize he was moved by her comment.

"I'm done," Christopher called out from the bathroom upstairs. "When is Sam coming home?"

Charlotte's mind slipped back into its worry cycle.

"I'm not sure," Charlotte called back, giving Bob another concerned glance.

Bob shook his head, as if to warn her not to get Christopher worried as well. She nodded her silent agreement and then trudged down the hallway and up the stairs, feeling every day of her age.

By the time Charlotte was upstairs, Christopher was already sitting in his bed, his hands folded. "I think our float will be the best," Christopher said with all the optimism of his young years. "Especially now that Grandpa is helping."

"And Uncle Pete and Dana."

Christopher wrinkled his nose. "Uncle Pete just argues with Grandpa."

"And how do you feel about that?" Charlotte asked, knowing how much Christopher disliked contention.

Christopher heaved a sigh and shook his head. "They don't listen to me, and it makes my stomach hurt."

This was something new. "I'll talk to them. Maybe they'll listen to *me*." She smoothed his hair back from his head. A few freckles already dotted his nose, and he had gained more color in his cheeks since school let out. "I'm glad you found something to keep you busy. It must be boring for you being here at home while Emily is at camp and Sam is working."

"It is. A little." Christopher pulled his knees up and wrapped his arms around them. "But Emily will be very surprised when she comes home and sees the float."

"Maybe she'll want to help out with it too," Charlotte offered.

"I wish Sam could help. I hope he comes home soon."

"I do too."

Christopher's expression brightened. "We're going to try to put the shed on the hay wagon tomorrow. Grandpa said we have to be very careful. Uncle Pete thinks it's going to fall apart into smithereens." Christopher frowned at that. "I was going to google the word *smithereens* to find out what it meant."

"Google?"

"You know. Look it up on the Internet."

"Well, I can tell you. It means lots of little pieces."

"How did you get to know that?"

"I've always known what smithereens meant." Charlotte pulled his quilt back as he slipped between the sheets. "Don't forget your prayers, young man," she said as she pushed herself up from the bed.

"I won't. And I'll pray that Sam will come home."

How did he know? Charlotte thought she had hidden her concern. She was about to reassure him when she saw the flare of lights in the yard.

Relief flooded her. Sam was home.

"Well, it looks like God answered your prayer even before you said it," she said, bending over to kiss her grandson good night. "And now, sleeping time."

Christopher grinned back at her, snuggling deeper into

his blankets. He gave a huge yawn and then curled up on his side. "Say hi to Sam for me, 'kay?"

"I will." Charlotte brushed a kiss over his forehead and then left his room.

But as she closed the door behind her, her relief at Sam's return was replaced with anger with her oldest grandson. How many times had they told him to call if he was going to be late or if he wasn't coming home?

How could he have been so selfish?

She caught herself as she walked down the stairs. Interesting how quickly worry was replaced with anger once she knew everything was fine.

"I think Sam is home," Bob said from the family room. "We'll have to have a talk with that boy."

"I know, I know," Charlotte said, bracing herself for what lay ahead.

The porch door opened and then closed quietly.

"Charlotte?" The voice was small, soft, and female.

It wasn't Sam. "Hannah?" Charlotte's heart raced in her chest as she hurried to the porch. "Hannah! What's wrong? Why are you here? Is Frank okay?" Hannah stood on the porch, leaning back against the door.

"Frank is fine," was all she said.

Charlotte felt as if she might have a heart attack herself. First her worry over Sam and then relief and then fear and now relief again. It was too hard on the poor ticker.

And now her worry over Sam had returned.

"You don't look too fine," Charlotte managed to say.

"Sam, what in the world were you thinking—" Bob cut his tirade off as soon as he too saw who stood in the porch. "Hannah! Where's Frank?"

"At home." Hannah looked from Bob to Charlotte, her eyes red-rimmed, as if she hadn't slept in days. "I've just come to borrow . . . can I borrow a cup of sugar?"

Charlotte shot a quick glance at the clock. Sugar? At ten o'clock at night?

"Of course you can. How's Frank?"

"Sleeping. He's fine."

Charlotte shot her husband a quick glance; Bob got the message. "I'll go over and sit with him."

"No. Really, you don't need to," Hannah said. "He's been sleeping really well on the oxygen. Much better than he was before." Hannah rubbed her eyes. "I just thought I would make a cake while he was resting, but then I ran out of sugar."

Charlotte frowned, puzzled at her friend's odd request. "I think you should at least sit down a minute. Have a cup of tea."

"I guess I could. I haven't started mixing up the cake yet." She trudged into the kitchen and sat down heavily at the kitchen table.

Charlotte's sympathy for her friend was followed by another stab of guilt. She shouldn't have listened to Hannah's protestations. She should have pushed past Hannah's stubbornness and helped her more after Frank came home.

"How are you feeling?" she asked as she filled the kettle with water.

Hannah sighed. "I'm fine."

Charlotte walked to the table, sat down across from Hannah, and took her hands between hers. "Are you sure?"

Hannah nodded but avoided Charlotte's eyes.

"I don't think you're telling me everything, and I don't believe you came all the way over here at this hour of the night just to tell me you're out of sugar."

Hannah blinked, and then to her surprise, Charlotte saw her friend's eyes fill with tears.

"You can tell me, you know," she urged. "You don't have to be so tough."

"I'm so tired," she said with a heavy sigh. "So exhausted."

"Why didn't you let me help you?" Charlotte stifled another stab of guilt.

Hannah sighed again. "Because that's not who I am. I'm the one who comes in and helps. I'm the one everyone depends on." Her voice broke, and Charlotte realized, to her shame, that she had thought the same. "I didn't want to admit that I need help."

"We can help you, Hannah."

"It's not just the help," Hannah said. "I'm scared. I keep hearing that concentrator hissing, and it reminds me of how sick Frank is. Then I get up and make sure it's still working right, and all I do is worry he might have another heart attack or that the concentrator will quit and he'll die... I can't face that, Charlotte. I can't lose him. I came so close. I just can't lose him."

Hannah looked as if she had aged ten years in the past few days.

Bob sat down with them, his presence a calming force on Hannah. "Have you talked to his doctor?" he asked.

Hannah nodded and pulled in a long, slow breath. "He keeps telling me that the oxygen is just a precaution. I know that, but things don't seem to be changing." Hannah pressed her arms closer to her chest, as if trying to contain her fear.

"If the doctor says he's doing okay, don't you think you should listen?" Bob suggested.

Charlotte shot him a glance as if to say, *You're not helping*. Bob returned her look with a frown; then he shrugged and retreated to the family room.

Obviously he thought his job here was done.

"Does Frank know how you feel?" Charlotte squeezed one of Hannah's hands and lowered it to her lap. She gently massaged it, as if, by her touch, she might smooth Hannah's concerns away.

"I can't tell him how scared I am. He needs me to be strong." Hannah sighed. "I think he doesn't want to admit it, but he's afraid too—which, in turn, makes me even more nervous. Frank has never been afraid of anything."

Charlotte hesitated, trying to find the right words. "I think sometimes we can feel as if we're caught on some kind of wave; we want to quit—we want to get out of the wave—but we can't, and that's what makes it really scary. You love Frank, and he needs your help. You have a job to do, and it's frightening. But what else can you do?"

Hannah's sigh came from her very soul. Her shoulders drooped, and her head fell as if she were withering under the truth Charlotte was placing on her.

"I know you're right, Charlotte. But, you know, you have Bob and the kids, and I'm mostly alone except for Frank."

Charlotte sighed. She'd never realized that Hannah felt so alone. She didn't know what else to say to encourage her friend. But she knew what else she could *do*. "Well, Hannah, please remember that you have us. How about we pray together?" Charlotte suggested.

Hannah nodded as Charlotte lowered her head and began. "Dear Lord, You know our hearts and our thoughts even before we know them ourselves. You know how Hannah is feeling right now. You know she's afraid. Lord, I pray You will still the storm of fear in Hannah's heart. That You will comfort her and give her strength to do her job. That she may know she's not alone in this. Amen."

She waited a moment, squeezing Hannah's hand again, and then she looked up.

A tear coursed down Hannah's cheek. "Thanks, Charlotte. I guess I was just feeling sorry for myself."

Charlotte gave her a gentle smile. "You are allowed to ask for help."

"I will. But not from you. You have enough to do."

Charlotte was about to protest just as the phone rang.

Charlotte's heart jumped. *Frank?*

She ran to take it, snatching it off the cradle. But it wasn't Frank.

"Mrs. Stevenson? This is Mr. Vance."

Charlotte frowned. She didn't recognize the name at all. "I'm sorry?" she said, her own heart settling down.

"My wife and I own a cabin at the lake. Unfortunately there was a party here tonight..."

Why was he telling her this?

"...and I have your grandson Sam here with me," he continued.

"Sam? Sam Slater is with you?" She pressed her hand to

her chest in relief. "Is he okay? I've been so worried. You have no idea what has been going through my head. Can I talk to him?"

"What you can do is come and get him. He and his friends have been drinking."

Charlotte reached blindly for the back of a chair, needing support. "Sam's been drinking? He's only eighteen."

"My point exactly. Now if you don't mind, we'd appreciate it if you'd come and get him. Otherwise we'll have to call the police, which is probably what we should have done anyway." Mr. Vance's voice was clipped. "This place is a disaster."

"What's going on, Charlotte? What's this about Sam?" Bob loomed over her, his face like a thundercloud.

She waved him off, still trying to assimilate the blow she'd just been dealt. "We'll come as soon as possible. What is your address?"

Mr. Vance gave it to her. "I want him gone in the next half hour. If you're not here, the next phone call I'm making is to the police."

Charlotte felt the sting of his words, as if it were her fault that her grandson had gotten himself in that condition. "There's no need for that, Mr. Vance. I will be leaving immediately."

"Make sure that happens." The sudden click in her ear was as loud as an explosion.

Charlotte's anger grew as she put the phone back on the cradle. Anger with her grandson for what he had done. Anger with Mr. Vance for being so rude.

But could she blame him? How would she react if she

came home and found eighteen-year-old kids drinking here on Heather Creek Farm?

Charlotte couldn't answer those questions.

"Charlotte, what's going on?" Bob demanded.

Charlotte pressed her fingers against her temples, massaging away the headache that was quickly making itself known. *Oh, Sam. How could you?*

Her anger with him was mixed with relief that he was still alive. And he hadn't eloped.

But he was in so much trouble.

She looked up at Bob, marshaling her own defenses. "I just got a call from a Mr. Vance. It seems there was a party at a cabin he and his wife own at the lake, and our Sam was there drinking."

Bob's eyes narrowed, and his hands clenched into fists at his sides. "Unbelievable." He was so livid that, for a moment, he couldn't say anything else.

He didn't need to.

"I have to go get him. If I'm not there in half an hour, Mr. Vance said he was calling the police." Charlotte got up slowly, in spite of the urgent threat hanging over them. She was suddenly weary. "Can you go start the car for me?"

"You're not going," Bob said, his eyes narrowed.

"But—"

"I'm going. And that's the end of that."

Bob grabbed the address and stomped to the porch, his footsteps ringing in the silence, the slam of the door bouncing off the walls.

"Grandma? What's happening?" Christopher stood in

the hallway, blinking at them. "I heard Grandpa yelling. Where is he going?"

"Oh, honey. You don't have to worry." Charlotte got up and hurried to her grandson's side. She pulled him close to her, hugging him.

"Why was Grandpa mad?"

Charlotte stroked Christopher's head, not sure what to tell him.

"I just got a call from a man. Sam is at his place."

"So Sam's okay?" Christopher looked up at her. "I don't have to pray for him anymore?"

Oh, you most certainly do.

Charlotte knelt down and squeezed his shoulders with her hands. "Grandpa is going to get him." She brushed a kiss over his head, wanting to pull him close, to cling to his simple purity. *Please, Lord, give us the wisdom to deal with this*, she prayed as she heard the roar of Bob's truck leaving the yard. *And keep Bob safe as he drives.*

"Can you tell Sam to come and say hi to me when he comes home?" Christopher asked.

"It will be awhile before Grandpa is back. You can talk to him tomorrow."

"Then I'll see him tomorrow." Christopher glanced past Charlotte to Hannah and tossed off a wave. "Hey, Mrs. Carter. Have a good sleep." And then he was gone, taking his innocence and purity with him.

Charlotte straightened, her knees creaking as she did. *I can't do this anymore*, she thought. *I just can't. Lord, this is too much.*

Then she glanced at Hannah, who had voiced almost the same thought only moments ago.

Hannah stared at Charlotte.

Charlotte walked toward her, wondering if her friend thought less of her now. "I'm sorry, but I can't come home with you as I'd like to do. Bob has to go get Sam, and I have to stay with Christopher."

"Of course you do." Hannah stood and gave Charlotte a wan smile. Then she reached out and pulled her close in a hug. "Thank you so much for listening. And for understanding."

"Don't be afraid to ask for help," Charlotte reminded her.

Hannah nodded. "I want you to know I'll be praying for you and Sam."

"I'm sorry you had to hear all this," Charlotte said, shame bringing heat to her cheeks.

"Charlotte, you are not the first parent—or grandparent, for that matter—to have to deal with this kind of thing, I'm sure. Now, can it be my turn to give some advice?" Hannah said quietly.

Charlotte nodded, her head now throbbing.

"Talk to him before you get angry with him. Find out what happened. Sam has done some silly things in the past, but each time it was a response to something that happened to him, or something he had to deal with. He's not a bad boy; he's just struggling. But you and Bob are doing a great job with him and the other children."

Charlotte's own tears threatened to fall as Hannah spoke. Hearing her friend praise her child-rearing abilities just as her husband was driving out to pick up their wayward grandson seemed ironic.

Yet she clung to the encouragement.

"Thank you, Hannah," she whispered.

Hannah patted her on the shoulder. "And please, promise me you'll talk to him first, okay?"

Charlotte looked up at her friend and smiled. "Okay. I will. If you promise me you'll let people help you."

Hannah gave a curt nod. "Okay. It's a deal. Now I'd better take my own advice and get back home. Thanks for listening. You are a good friend."

Charlotte smiled at how quickly her friend's resolve had returned. "Thanks for coming over. I think God knew I needed you here when I got that phone call."

"Funny how things work out." Hannah gave her another smile, said good-bye, and left.

As Hannah drove away, Charlotte trudged to the family room, fell into her recliner, and laid her aching head back.

"Please, Lord, be with Hannah and Frank. And give us wisdom to deal with Sam when he comes home," Charlotte prayed out loud. She waited a moment and then added, "And please don't let Bob yell at him when he picks him up."

Charlotte waited a moment, as if unsure of what to pray for next. She thought of Christopher sleeping upstairs, eager to see his big brother. What would he think when he found out? Should they tell him?

Her mind slipped from him to Emily at Bible camp. She sent up a prayer for her as well, praying that the camp had been meaningful to her. That she would come back with an awareness of faith and what God could do in her life.

From there she moved on to Anna and Bill and their children. Then to Pete and Dana. As her prayers wove around her family, Charlotte felt God's peace slowly embracing and enfolding her.

She and Bob were not alone in this business. Every step of the way, God was with them, behind them, and beside them.

Slowly, as she prayed, sleep drifted over her.

Chapter Seventeen

Sam opened his eyes and looked around his room, trying to get his bearings. Then, slowly, recognition dawned, and Sam groaned. The events of last night came crashing into his mind, and he groaned again.

How could he have been so incredibly stupid? Like a horror show, scenes from last night ran through his head. Arielle breaking up with him. His anger and the party he immediately headed for. The beer, which he didn't even enjoy. Then a sudden shout. Everyone scattering. Somehow getting left behind and ending up with a very angry Mr. Vance yelling at him.

Then, even worse, Grandpa coming to get him, too angry to say anything to him. Finally getting home and hearing Grandma and Grandpa saying they were going to have a talk with him first thing this morning.

It took him forever to fall asleep. He wished they would have just gotten the lecture over and done with last night, but Christopher was up, and Sam suspected they didn't want to talk in front of him.

"Sam, are you up?" Grandma's voice came from outside his door.

"Yeah," he muttered, very slowly pushing himself upright. "I'm up."

"Get dressed and come downstairs. We need to talk."

Here it comes. He knew he was in big, deep, unavoidable trouble.

He got dressed and washed up. Then he took a breath and walked down the stairs to face the music.

Grandma sat at one end of the table; Grandpa sat at the other end, a cup of coffee in front of him.

"Where's Christopher?" Sam mumbled, grabbing the back of a chair and pulling it out. He sat down and took a breath, readying himself for whatever Grandma and Grandpa would see fit to dole out.

"He's outside with Uncle Pete and Aunt Dana working on the float," Grandma said, her voice quiet. "So now we can talk."

A thick and heavy silence followed that comment.

"What were you thinking?" Grandpa finally asked, his voice full of the disappointment Sam knew he would be feeling.

Sam rubbed at his eyes with his fingers and then released a sigh. "I'm sorry. I was stupid."

"Do you have any idea how humiliating it was for me to go to the Vances' cabin to pick you up?"

Sam winced at the anger in Grandpa's voice. "I'm so sorry, Grandpa. I'm so sorry," he said, not wanting to look up and see the disappointment in their faces.

"Why did you go to that party?" Grandma asked, her voice still quiet. "I thought you were supposed to go out with Arielle?"

"I thought so too," Sam said, still looking down at his hands resting on the table. "But she broke up with me. That's why I went."

"That's no excuse," Grandpa said. "No excuse for what you did."

"I'm not trying to make excuses," Sam mumbled. "I know what I did was stupid. I know I was wrong." And he could kiss good-bye any chance of getting back together with Arielle again.

"Why didn't you call us and tell us where you were?" Grandma's voice was full of concern.

Which made him feel even worse.

"Arielle broke up with me while I was on my cell phone driving home from work in River Bend. I got mad and... well... I pitched the phone across a field."

"Do you know where it is?"

Sam slowly shook his head.

"You'll have to go look for it, and if you can't find it you'll have to cancel your plan. If someone finds it and starts using it, you'll have a huge bill to pay," Grandma said.

Grandpa leaned back in his chair heaving a heavy sigh. "So now we have to figure out what to do. First off, I want you to write a letter of apology to Mr. and Mrs. Vance. I'll take you over there this morning to get your car; you can give them the letter and ask if you can help them clean up their place." Grandpa tapped one hand against his arm.

Sam lifted his head in surprise. "I wasn't the only one there... I didn't throw the party." A dozen more protests clamored to be spoken, but at the thunderous expression on Grandpa's face, he stopped himself.

"How the other parents decide to deal with their children is up to them, but this is what your grandmother and I decided should be done."

Sam glanced at Grandma, who sat in her chair, her arms folded over her chest, looking down. As if she couldn't look him in the eye.

"You'll be phoning Uncle Bill to tell him why you won't be coming in to work today, and then you had better get to work on that letter so I can take you back to the Vances'," Grandpa said.

His voice was a little quieter now. He stood and then slowly pushed his chair back under the table, as if it were too much work for him. "I'll drop you off, and you can drive your car home when you're done helping them clean up."

Sam had nothing to say. He knew he had messed up, and he knew he had to be punished. He got up and went to the phone to get the first part of his punishment over and done with.

"I'M LEAVING FOR BEDFORD to get Emily," Charlotte called up to Bob, who stood on the hay wagon struggling to move the plow Christopher insisted be part of the float.

"Is Slurpin' Slater back from the Vance place yet?" Pete asked from beside the ramshackle shed they had managed to move onto the hay wagon.

Charlotte shot him an admonishing glance. Pete seemed to think there was some humor in the situation that Charlotte hadn't found. She turned to Bob.

"If Sam gets home before I do, tell him I need to talk to him. I've got a list of chores as long as my arm that I want him to do."

Pete snorted. "Oh, c'mon, Mom. It was just a party."

"Pete. We're not talking about that." Charlotte angled her head toward Christopher, who was watching the exchange with an avid look on his face. Christopher had no idea what had happened, and Charlotte didn't want him to know what his older brother had been up to.

"Of course we're not. Because I don't have an opinion on that," Pete snapped.

Charlotte frowned at the cynical tone threaded through Pete's voice. What was that about?

But she didn't have time to talk to him, especially not with Christopher around. She got into the car, and as she started it, a sigh drifted between her lips.

What was she going to do about Sam? Making him write the letter and help clean up the mess was a good start. But what else?

When would he learn? When would he grow up? How could she teach him good judgment?

Charlotte tried to push away the panic clawing at her. Before she knew it, he would be out of the house. Then whatever opportunity they had to teach him anything would be over. Would there be enough time?

She thought about Bob saying he didn't want to have the regrets Frank was feeling. Had she and Bob done enough for the kids? And what about Emily and Christopher? Would they also disappoint her and Bob?

The questions, the same ones that had kept her up most

of the night, twisted and spun through her head, guilt floating in their wake.

Please, Lord, help me to trust in You, she prayed as she drove toward the church. *Help us to know that You love these children even more than we do. That they are Yours first and ours second. Help us to do what we can and then to let go.*

It was that last part that was the hardest. That last part was the thing she had struggled with so mightily after Denise left those many years ago, trusting God to watch over the children when they were no longer around. Now that Sam was getting older, she was increasingly aware that time seemed to be running out on her opportunities to guide the children.

As Charlotte turned into the church parking lot, she felt a gentle lift of anticipation. She had missed Emily the last ten days and was looking forward to seeing her again.

Young voices rang out as Charlotte got out of the car. Sleeping bags, backpacks, and suitcases lay piled up with no apparent regard for order or neatness, in much the same way they had been when she first dropped Emily off.

Charlotte walked slowly to where the bus was parked, looking over the bedlam of bodies that didn't seem in any rush to dissipate. The noise reminded her of the chickens when they had been disturbed.

"Grandma! There you are." Emily's voice rang out over the cacophony.

Charlotte glanced around, trying to find her granddaughter. Then there she was, running toward her, arms wide.

Charlotte had to look twice; then she was enveloped in a huge, tight hug.

"I'm glad to be home," Emily said, giving Charlotte an extra squeeze.

Charlotte recovered quickly enough to return the hug, surprise mixing with pleasure at Emily's exuberance. She pulled back and held her granddaughter by the shoulders. "Look at you," Charlotte gushed. Camp had obviously agreed with her. Indeed, her granddaughter looked tanned and happy; her hair shone, and her eyes sparkled.

"I had such a great time," Emily said, dropping her arm over Charlotte's shoulders. Charlotte couldn't believe Emily was nearly the same height she was.

Charlotte slipped her arm around her granddaughter's waist, pushing aside the thought that someday Emily would be leaving Heather Creek as well. "How was camp?" she asked as they walked back toward the bus.

"I met so many interesting people and had such fun. I went canoeing, did crafts, went for nature walks, and didn't get any sleep at all." Emily's wide yawn underscored that last comment.

"I'm sure you'll be catching up once we're home."

"No doubt." Another yawn followed that statement.

Young kids Charlotte didn't recognize greeted Emily as they got to the bus. Some kids from the church waved. Emily introduced Charlotte to a few, her arm still slung over Charlotte's shoulder as they wove their way through the crowd. Which continued to surprise Charlotte. She thought that as soon as they got closer to her friends, Emily would pull away from her. But she didn't. Her granddaughter was maturing—and growing up in so many other ways as well.

"Here's my stuff." Emily bent over and picked up her backpack and suitcase. Charlotte got the sleeping bag.

"Hey, Emily. See you later," Ashley called through the window of her mother's car.

"Later," Emily replied, throwing a wave to her friend. She paused a moment, glancing around, and Charlotte wondered if she was looking for Troy. Charlotte caught a flicker of worry passing over her granddaughter's face and wondered if something had happened between them. But as quickly as it came, the worry left.

Then Emily slung her backpack over her shoulder and groaned. "I've got a ton of laundry to do as soon as we get home."

"And don't forget the sleeping," Charlotte teased as they walked back to the car. They got in, and with a squeal, Emily snatched up the cell phone waiting for her on the car seat. Charlotte had figured she would want it as soon as possible so she had brought it along.

Before Charlotte even had the car in gear, Emily was busily texting, the worry on her face returning as she hurriedly pressed the keys.

"Did you get a lot of messages while you were gone?" Charlotte asked, glancing at her granddaughter, amazed at how quickly her thumbs flew over the tiny keyboard. Could anything coherent come out of that flurry of activity?

"Not as many as I would have liked," Emily said with a frown.

"I'm glad you enjoyed camp," Charlotte said.

Emily glanced up from her texting and nodded. "Yeah. It was kind of weird at first, but I learned a lot."

"About...?"

"Life. God. Forgiveness." Emily gave her a grin, her other annoyance seemingly forgotten for now. "Actually, the focus was on sharing our burdens and putting them in God's hands. Kind of a freeing thought," Emily mused.

Charlotte felt a glow of happiness at Emily's words. And behind the glow came a reminder of her prayer only a few moments ago. Her granddaughter was truly growing up.

"Sometimes we take on burdens we don't have to," Charlotte agreed, her words reminding her of her struggles with Sam. And of Hannah's with Frank. "I think we all struggle with one kind of guilt or another. Sometimes it's guilt we take on; sometimes it's guilt we should be aware of."

She waited to see what Emily would say, but when she got no response she looked over at her granddaughter and then smiled.

Emily was fast asleep.

"I REALLY THINK we should put the plow farther back and the shed at the front," Grandpa was saying.

Christopher looked at the plow and then shook his head. "No. We're trying to tell the story of the bread. So first we plow the field, and then we plant it, and then we beat the wheat, and then we grind the flour for the bread."

"Now we're telling a story?" Grandpa asked, pulling his cap off with one hand and scratching his head with the other. "I thought we were just trying to figure out how to use some of the old stuff."

"Telling a story was the whole point of the float."

Christopher sighed. He thought he had explained this enough, but obviously Grandpa didn't get it. "And to tell the story right, everything has to be in the right order."

"But the plow is too heavy for the front," Grandpa said.

"I think we should move it to the middle," Uncle Pete put in, getting up from the back of the float. "It's way bigger than the flail."

"Then we'll need someone to operate the flail," Grandpa said.

"That would be too dangerous. We can just hang it up," Pete replied. He sounded peeved with Grandpa.

"Do you think people will know what it is if you do that?" Grandpa frowned.

"Who cares? It's just a float."

"If we're doing this job, we should do it well," Grandpa said. He let go of the handles of the plow and stood, glaring at Uncle Pete.

"And there's also the case for return on investment."

"Whatever that means," Grandpa groused.

Christopher glanced from Uncle Pete to Grandpa and tried not to get nervous. He didn't like the way they were fighting. If Uncle Pete got mad enough, he would leave.

"It means that the end result of a project has to be worth the input."

Uncle Pete had dropped his hammer and was glaring back at Grandpa. Christopher glanced from Grandpa to Uncle Pete, trying to think of a way to get them to stop fighting.

"If we had someone to use the flail, *then* do you think it would look okay?" Christopher asked, trying to get them back on the topic.

"I'm driving the tractor," Grandpa said.

And he was standing at the plow. Christopher glanced over at Uncle Pete. Maybe he would change his mind.

"Forget it, Christopher," Uncle Pete said, holding his hands up. "I'm only doing what I'm doing because Dana asked me to."

"Do you think Sam would do it?" Christopher asked.

"Sam is in enough trouble as it is," Grandpa snapped.

"Whatever that has to do with anything," Uncle Pete said back.

"He has to be punished. And you know it."

"Boys will be boys."

"That's no excuse. It wasn't for you and Bill, and it isn't for him."

What were they talking about? No one would tell him anything. The only thing he knew was that Sam looked extra grumpy when he got up this morning so there was no way Christopher was going to ask *him*.

"I think we should get Slurpin' Slater to handle the flail," Pete said. "It would be good punishment for him. If that's what you're thinking of doing."

"That's enough, Pete." Now Grandpa really sounded angry, and Christopher wondered again what in the world was going on. Everyone seemed angry with Sam, but no one would say why. And it seemed, because of that, Grandpa and Uncle Pete were angry with each other. Of course, lately, Grandpa and Uncle Pete were always mad at each other. Ever since the mix-up about spraying the field with the wrong chemicals.

"We could hang it up on something," Christopher said.

"Then people can see it. Maybe make a sign so people know."

"Sam's been doing really good," Uncle Pete said, like he was going back to what they were talking about before. "I think you've got to give him some credit for that. And it's not like he hurt anyone or—"

"Pete. That's enough." Now Grandpa was really mad, and Christopher was getting more and more frustrated. They needed to work on the float, not fight with each other. If Grandpa and Uncle Pete kept at it, one of them would stomp away mad, and then the other one would leave and Christopher would be left trying to figure out how he could finish the float.

The sound of a car made everyone look up.

"Hey, Grandma is here with Emily!" Christopher jumped off the float and ran to the car, only too glad to leave Grandpa and Uncle Pete behind for now.

"Hey, everyone," Emily said as she got out of the car. She hugged Christopher and then Grandpa, who pulled back and ruffled Emily's hair.

"You look like you've been outside, missy," he said, grinning at her.

"I probably look like I need a shower."

Uncle Pete pretended to sniff her and then wrinkled his nose. "You not only *look* like you need a shower, Buttercup..."

Emily punched his arm and then gave Aunt Dana a hug. "Get any more done on the house while I was gone?"

"We're waiting for the electricians to finish," Uncle Pete said.

"Grandpa, Uncle Pete, and Aunt Dana are helping me make a float," Christopher said, trying to catch Emily's attention. "And we need one more person to operate the flail." Maybe Emily would help out.

Emily smiled as if she knew exactly what he wanted to ask her. "I'm so tired. I can't imagine working on the float."

So much for *that* idea.

"I still think Slurpin' Slater should help," Uncle Pete said.

"Slurpin' Slater? Who's that?" Emily asked.

"It's your uncle's ridiculous nickname for Sam. And we're not using it anymore." Grandma gave Uncle Pete her *I mean business* look that could really make Christopher nervous; but Uncle Pete just grinned.

"Why that nickname?" Emily asked.

Uncle Pete was just about to say something when the sound of Sam's car made everyone stop talking.

Sam pulled up beside Grandma's car, looking even more grumpy than he had when he got up this morning. He turned off the car and stayed inside, staring straight ahead for a bit, as if he didn't want to look at anybody.

Uncle Pete gave another snort, walked around to Sam's side of the car, and opened the door. "Hey, mister, you're helping us. That's part of your punishment."

"I know, I know." Sam got out of the car and blew out his breath.

"Punishment?" Emily asked. "For what?"

Christopher wanted to know too, but Sam looked at Christopher and then back at Emily and shook his head. Christopher knew what that meant: *not in front of Christopher.*

Sometimes that made him so mad. They treated him like he was a little kid or something.

"Did you get the letter delivered?" Grandpa was asking Sam.

So that's why Sam had to leave so early this morning. But where had he delivered a letter? And why?

"I did." Sam sounded mad again.

"How did it go?" Grandma asked.

Sam pressed his lips together and then turned to Grandma and Grandpa. "I was the only kid who came back. The only one out of all seventeen or eighteen kids who came back and apologized."

"You can be proud of that," Grandma was saying.

"Hard to be proud when I was also the one who got the whole load. They were angry with me when it was their own daughter who invited everyone. They acted like I was the only one who'd had something to—"

"Sam!" Grandpa stopped him, and Christopher wondered why.

"See? That's what I'm talking about," Uncle Pete said. "We can't even mention the word. Goodness, can we get some reality here?"

"This is none of your business," Grandpa snapped.

"But it is, you know," Uncle Pete snapped back.

"Can someone please tell me what is going on?" Emily asked, raising her voice over Uncle Pete's and Grandpa's yelling.

Everyone was quiet after Emily's question, and Christopher guessed no one wanted to say anything in front of him.

Then everyone looked at him. Did they want him to go so they could yell some more?

"I think we can talk about this party while we're all congregated here with our mouths open like a bunch of guppies," Uncle Pete said.

"Pete. Mind your tongue."

"Party? Slurpin' Slater? What in the world is going on that Christopher and I don't know about?" Emily asked.

"I had a beer at a party last night," Sam finally said.

Christopher didn't understand. Sam wouldn't drink, would he?

"It was stupid and dumb, and I shouldn't have done it, and I apologized all over creation and ended up humiliating myself in front of the Vances." Sam looked at Emily, which made Christopher even more curious.

"Why did you do that, Sam?" Emily asked. Now she was mad at him too.

"Hey, cut me a break, would you? Arielle had just broken up with me, and I had nowhere else to go and I was upset and I just showed up. I wasn't going to stay but I did, and I don't know how many times I have to tell everyone I am sorry and I'll never do it again and on and on..."

"Arielle broke up with you?" Emily sounded shocked; Christopher was too. They had been so happy that Arielle and Sam were back together again. And so was Sam. He'd been whistling again, which usually meant he was feeling good.

"That is still no excuse," Grandpa added. "What you did was wrong."

"I come back from camp, from a really great experience,

and all this is going on? What kind of family is this?" Emily sounded upset.

"Don't get all holier than thou on us," Sam snapped back. "Just 'cause you were at Bible camp doesn't make you better."

"Sam, watch your tone," Grandma was saying. She had her hand on Grandpa's arm like she was holding him back, and she was looking from Emily to Sam to Pete.

"I'm not holier than thou, but I learned a few things," Emily said, staring at Sam. "And drinking wasn't one of them."

"Of course, you would never do anything wrong, would you, Emily? You and Troy have such a perfect relationship."

"What are you saying?" Now Emily sounded mad, and Christopher was getting more and more confused.

"I'm not saying anything, just reminding you that your boyfriend wasn't always the knight in shining armor you seem to think he is now."

"Hey, would you two just chill?" Uncle Pete said with a loud voice.

Christopher's stomach was starting to hurt. No one was looking at him or talking to him. They were all too busy yelling at each other.

And he was mad too. He was tired of being ignored. Of being treated like he didn't matter.

"Stop arguing," he said. But his voice was so small, he didn't think anyone heard him. He tried again, wishing they would all stop. Wishing they would just get along.

His stomach made a funny flop, and he swallowed hard.

Then he swallowed again as everyone kept talking over each other. He didn't like how everyone sounded. Didn't like how angry everyone was.

His chest got tight, and he felt like something was pinching his forehead. He blinked, squeezing his eyes shut. Then again. Why was everything turning such a funny color, like it was yellow around the edges?

His ears were humming, and he couldn't get enough air.

Then he heard someone calling his name from far, far away.

And then it was like he was falling backward into blackness.

Chapter Eighteen

"Christopher, honey. Talk to me." Charlotte pressed a cold facecloth to Christopher's forehead. Drips of water ran down his face, making dark tracks through the dust on his cheeks.

Christopher blinked and then tried to sit up, looking around wildly.

"What happened? What did I do?" The anguish in his voice cut Charlotte to the core.

"Nothing. Nothing at all." Emily was on the other side, holding Christopher's hand.

"You fainted, sweetheart," Charlotte said, wiping the rest of his face.

Christopher looked disgusted. "Only girls faint."

Charlotte's laugh was weak with relief. "No. Grown men faint too."

Her heart was still pounding out an erratic rhythm. When she heard his small cry she had turned in time to see his eyes roll up in his head. Then his knees buckled and he crumpled to the ground, and Charlotte's heart jumped into her throat.

The arguments that had been flying back and forth over the yard had come to a crashing halt.

And so they should have.

Charlotte suspected it was those very arguments that had caused Christopher's distress.

"Why did you faint, son?" Bob was asking, hovering behind Charlotte. "Was it too hot?"

"I don't think so." Christopher struggled to sit up and then reached out to Charlotte when he wavered.

"Just rest, sweetie," Charlotte said, settling down on the ground and supporting her grandson against her. She pressed a kiss to his warm, sticky hair, relief following on the heels of her concern.

Pete, Bob, Sam, and Emily stood around, fidgeting as if they were unsure of what to do or say.

"What happened?" Sam was asking.

Christopher swallowed and then frowned. "I dunno. When all you guys were yelling at each other my stomach got all funny feeling, and then it was like everything got black."

"We weren't yelling at each other," Pete said.

Christopher looked down.

"Yes, you were," he mumbled, his hands twisting the edge of his T-shirt. "You were all yelling at each other, and it made me feel really funny. I hate it when you fight and yell. We're a family, and we're supposed to love each other." He sniffed and then wiped the tears away with one hand. "And I'm not crying, so don't call me a baby."

No one said anything for a long while.

Toby, curious about the commotion, had wandered over and now laid her head on Christopher's leg. Her soft brown eyes looked up at him as if to offer some comfort.

"You were the only one who wasn't mad, Toby," Christopher said quietly, stroking the dog's dark brown fur.

Charlotte looked up at her family, all gathered around. In their faces she saw mixtures of shame, embarrassment, and concern.

Sam was the first one to kneel down in front of his little brother. "I'm so sorry, Christopher," he said quietly, stroking Toby as well. "It's all my fault. I did something stupid, and everyone is upset."

Bob laid his hand on Sam's shoulder. "I'm sorry too," he said, both to Christopher and to Sam. "I should have listened to you. You made a mistake, but you owned up to it, and that's important."

"And I should have kept my nose out of it all," Pete said.

"And I shouldn't have come across as so righteous," Emily added, kneeling down beside Sam and Christopher. She put her arms around both her brothers' shoulders and squeezed. "We need each other. We have to help each other, and I'm sorry."

"And I'm sorry that I didn't stop things sooner," Charlotte said.

Bob gave her a tender smile. "Now, Charlotte," he said quietly, "don't think you have to be the one to fix everything."

Charlotte smiled at his assessment even as part of her wanted to protest that he was wrong. She knew that he was right. She was usually the one to interfere. The one to make things right. As if by her actions alone people would change.

Charlotte looked around her family, feeling the anger,

frustration, and sorrow she had noted in such an abundance only a few moments ago melt away in the warmth of the love her family now poured out to each other.

And how had it happened? Was it anything she did? Was it anything anyone else did?

No, it was the distress of this innocent boy that had made them all realize what they were doing to each other.

Christopher sniffed, still looking down at Toby, still stroking her soft fur. "I don't like it when we fight," he said quietly, his voice still shaky. "We're supposed to love each other. Like Jesus loves us."

Charlotte smiled and gave him a quick hug. "You are absolutely right," she said. "Jesus wants us to remember that He loves all of us the same."

"Yeah, like we learned at camp, we should try to see Jesus in each other," Emily said quietly. She looked over at Sam. "I'm sorry, Sam. I shouldn't have judged you."

He shook his head. "Well, while I'm at it, I'm sorry I said what I did. I shouldn't have—"

"Doesn't matter," Emily said. "We can catch up later."

Sam glanced over at her and then nodded, sharing a smile with her that made Charlotte realize they had their own relationship—their own secrets and things they talked about away from the adults. Things they could encourage each other about. They didn't need her input.

And while it made her feel a little odd, it was, at the same time, very freeing. Raising the kids wasn't entirely up to her or Bob. God had his own ways of dealing with them and supporting them.

Pete ran his forefinger alongside his nose, looking

uncomfortable. "So, this love fest is all well and good, but we do have a float to make, don't we?"

Sam got up. "That's right. We should get at it. We only have a week."

"What do you want me to do, Christopher?" Emily asked.

Christopher blinked as he looked around the group. "You mean you all want to help me?" He sounded so dumbfounded and so happy, Charlotte had to resist the urge to pull him close into another tight hug of reassurance. Instead she made do with smoothing his hair back from his face. "I think we all should help."

Christopher got up and brushed the dust off his pants. He put his hands on his hips and stared them all down. "But we're not allowed to fight. And I mean it."

Pete looked taken aback. "What's the fun of that?" he said with mock horror.

Charlotte frowned at him, and he winked in return. Marriage was mellowing him somewhat, but he was still Pete.

"Okay," Pete said, adjusting his cap on his head. "We won't fight."

"And you'll have to listen to me," Christopher said, seeming to realize that, for now, he had an advantage and he needed press it.

"Aye, aye, sir," Pete gave him a mock salute.

"Okay." Christopher took a deep breath. "Let's go."

Christopher led the way, followed by Sam and Emily, with Bob and Pete behind them.

Charlotte watched them walk across the yard, amazed at how quickly things had changed. Half an hour ago anger and frustration bounced among her family members. Now, duly chastened by the youngest person in the family, they were willing to work together. To help each other.

Thank You, Lord, for my family, she prayed, wrapping her sweater around her. *Help them to always realize how much we need each other. How much we depend on each other. Help them always to see Jesus in each other.*

She walked back to the house, already planning dinner.

Help me not to think that I always need to solve everything. And help me to remember that You can use a little child like Christopher just as easily as You can use me.

"SAM, MAY I TALK TO YOU?" Uncle Bill said from the doorway of the coffee room on Friday afternoon.

Sam jumped, almost dumping the water he was pouring into the coffeemaker. He finished the job, being extra careful not to spill anything. Then he wiped his sweaty palms against the sides of his pants and turned to face his uncle.

This is it, he thought. *This is where I get fired.* He was pretty sure Grandma or Grandpa or maybe both of them had talked to Uncle Bill about the party he'd gone to. About the few drinks he'd had.

"Sure. What can I do for you?" Sam tried to sound calm, but inside he was nervous. Uncle Bill had his lawyer face on, and when he did that he could look pretty intimidating.

"In my office, please." Then he turned without another word and walked away.

Sam followed him, feeling like a convict going to his doom. Lena looked up as he passed and gave him an encouraging smile, which wasn't really encouraging at all. Sam decided it looked more like she felt sorry for him.

Uncle Bill closed the door of the office behind him. "Sit down, Sam."

Sam did, perching himself on the edge of the chair as Uncle Bill sat down across from him, pulling a file toward him. A clock ticked in the silence, and on the other side of the door, Sam heard the muffled ringing of a phone. Uncle Bill turned a couple of pages, frowning as if looking for something specific.

Sam couldn't stand it anymore. "Is this where you say I'm fired?"

Uncle Bill glanced up. "Pardon me?"

"I know I've messed up in all kinds of ways, both here at work and at home, so I'm guessing you want to fire me."

Uncle Bill sat back in his chair, and the faint smile tugging on his mouth gave Sam a tiny bit of hope. "No, Sam. I'm not firing you."

"In spite of what Mrs. Pictou thinks?"

"Mrs. Pictou is a very precise and conscientious employee," Uncle Bill said. "I know it seems she's been hard on you, but I think she was just trying to bring you up to her standards." Uncle Bill hesitated a moment. "Plus I think she had someone else in mind for your position when I mentioned that I was looking for a filing clerk."

Sam thought about the bits and pieces of the conversation he'd overheard last week. "Her son?" he guessed.

"You weren't supposed to know that, but yes."

"I kind of heard her talking the other day."

"I'm not surprised," he thought he heard his uncle

murmur. But then Uncle Bill leaned forward, looking at the file on his desk again. "However, her opinion is not what I wish to discuss. I want to talk to you about something else that your grandmother has brought to my attention."

Sam groaned. He *was* getting fired.

"I know that I don't have kids your age, but at one time, believe it or not, I *was* your age. And I know how easy it is to get caught up in the wrong crowd."

Sam couldn't help a beat of frustration. "It's not like I got drunk or anything. Grandma and Grandpa overreacted."

"Why do you think that?"

Sam shrugged. "Well, it's not like I was drunk..."

"But it *is* illegal for you to be drinking, yes?"

Sam couldn't say anything to that.

Uncle Bill turned more pages of the file on his desk. "You know what I have here?"

Sam shook his head.

"It's a case I'm representing. It involves a young man, a year older than you, who was drinking. He obviously didn't think drinking was a big deal either because after the party where he wasn't supposed to be drinking, he got in his car." Uncle Bill paused as he lifted another page.

"I'm representing the family of the young girl who was injured as a result of the crash that young man caused—a young girl who will have to deal with the repercussions of his carelessness for the rest of her life." Uncle Bill glanced up at Sam. "All because one young man wanted to have fun that he, and I quote, 'didn't think was such a big deal.'"

Sam looked down at his hands, feeling lower than a snake.

"He didn't think he was impaired, according to the police reports, even though he blew over the limit." Though Uncle Bill spoke quietly, each word hit Sam a bit harder. "He made a decision that not only affected the family of the girl but also gave him the permanent knowledge that his choices—the choices he thought were no big deal—hurt an innocent person. This case will take time, and it will take its toll on many people in many ways."

With a creak of his chair, Uncle Bill sat back. He didn't say anything more, and Sam didn't know what to say.

Silence filled the office and Sam squirmed. "I'm sorry." He fiddled with the button on his cuff, not sure what to say or do.

"You don't have to apologize to me. I understand that you went back to help clean up, which I think is admirable." Uncle Bill rocked in his chair, and Sam finally dared to look up. His uncle was smiling. "I didn't want to lecture you because I think you're a bad person, Sam. I know you haven't had the guidance you should have had, but at the same time, I think you have the potential to be a good young man. I've been pleased with your work here, and your work ethic, the past two weeks. As I said, I see a lot of potential in you and think you could go far."

Uncle Bill leaned forward, and although Sam was encouraged by what he was saying, he was wondering how much longer his uncle would talk to him. Once Uncle Bill got going...

"Anyhow, I don't want to go on and on." Uncle Bill gave him a quick smile, which made Sam squirm again. Could Uncle Bill read his mind? "But I did want to speak to you about choices and the repercussions of some of those choices. Do you understand?"

Sam nodded. "Yeah. I do. I never stopped to think about what could happen."

"Most people don't, Sam. And that's how tragedies occur." He got up from his desk; Sam guessed the lecture was over.

"I . . . uh . . . thanks for talking to me."

Uncle Bill grinned. "That's what family is for."

Sam grinned back, feeling surprisingly comfortable now that the talk was over. "I guess so."

Uncle Bill shot a quick glance at the clock, which was Sam's cue to get up and get back to work. But just before he got to the door he turned. "Thanks again for the job. I'm really enjoying the work. It's getting more interesting."

"Like any job, it has its tedious moments, but overall, the legal field is an important one with many options and opportunities." Uncle Bill nodded at him and smiled.

Sam stepped out of the office and closed the door behind him. Lena, Uncle Bill's secretary, looked up from her computer as he passed her. "How did it go?"

"Pretty good, I think." A little uncomfortable, but Sam didn't want to tell her that.

"He's pretty pleased with your work, you know," Lena said.

Though Uncle Bill had said as much to him, hearing it secondhand made it seem more real. "Thanks. That's good to know."

As he went back to work, he felt just a bit freer, a bit lighter on his feet. And, in spite of losing Arielle and the whole mess of the last couple of days, a little happier.

EMILY LOOKED OVER at the phone and sighed. She should call Troy. She hadn't called him since she got back yesterday. He had known she was coming back Thursday, yet she hadn't worked up the courage to call him because she was sure he knew everything that had happened at camp. She was also sure that Nicole had twisted things around to make her and Mike's relationship seem different than it was.

"What's wrong?" Grandma asked, looking up from the material she was cutting out.

"Nothing." Emily turned back to the sewing machine and picked up the pieces of the costume she would wear on Christopher's float. She started sewing. Then the bobbin jammed, and she slammed her hand against the machine. "Why do I even bother?" she grumbled, yanking the material out from under the presser foot and slicing at the threads with the scissors.

"Careful, missy. You're going to cut your hand," Grandma warned.

Emily threw the partially sewn costume down on the table and bunched the material in her hands. "I don't think I'll get this done in time," she said, frustration filling her voice. "It's just not working out. It's not going the way I want it to."

Grandma put down her scissors and came over to Emily. She carefully took the costume from her hands.

"Somehow I get the feeling it's not the dress that's the problem," she said.

Emily shoved her hands through her hair and sighed again. "No. You're right. It's not."

Grandma sat down beside her and gently turned her face up to hers. "Can you tell me what is?"

Emily heard the sympathy in her voice, and yet she hesitated.

"Is it about Troy?"

Emily nodded.

"Can you tell me?"

Emily looked up at her grandmother, and as she looked into Grandma's eyes, she knew *she* would understand. So she took a deep breath and started at the beginning. She told her everything. Told her about Nicole. About Mike. How she and Mike had talked, how Mike had saved her life. About their kiss on the dock. And how she was worried that Nicole had already talked to Troy about what she had seen.

"Have you talked to Troy since you got back?" Grandma asked her when she was done.

"I don't dare."

"He has called here a few times," Grandma reminded her.

"I know. But I'm scared."

"Of what?"

"Of what he will think of me."

"But you won't know what he thinks until you talk to him, right?"

That made sense, but it was also very scary. "I suppose."

"If you really care for him like you say you do, then you need to sit down and tell him for yourself what happened and why. Tell him like you told me. Then, if he really cares for you, he'll understand that nothing happened. And if he doesn't understand, then maybe he's not the one for you."

Emily swallowed a knot of nervousness. "I suppose."

"Bedford isn't that big. You'll have to face him sooner or later. So you may as well make it on your own terms."

Which also made sense.

"Why don't you let me finish this costume? You can call him and make arrangements to meet him in town."

Emily glanced at the phone and realized that Grandma was right.

She called him, and when she got his voice mail she took a chance and left a message asking him to meet her at Mel's in half an hour.

Twenty minutes later she was sitting at Mel's, a soft drink in her hands, staring out the window, jumping every time she saw a dark truck. She didn't know if he would come or not, but she knew she had to take the chance.

She'd dressed carefully. Over a T-shirt, she'd pulled on a favorite shirt, one she'd pieced together from three others. It was funky and fun, and reflected her style.

The door of the diner opened, and Emily's heart jumped again—and then fell with a thud.

Nicole!

Seriously?

Was there no place she could go without running into the girl?

Emily spun her head away, and was thankful that Nicole walked right by without noticing her. Then, before the bell over Mel's door even finished jangling, the door opened again.

And there stood Troy.

Emily's heart skipped in her chest, and in that moment

she knew that what she felt for Troy was completely different from anything she'd experienced with Mike.

He looked around the diner, caught her gaze, and walked toward her, his eyes on her. "Hey, beautiful," he said as he sat down. "I missed you."

Emily released the breath she didn't even know she'd been holding. "I missed you too." She reached across the table to take his hand. "How have you been?"

"Good. Good. Better now that you're here." He pushed his hair away from his face, his smile warming her heart. "How was camp?"

Did she imagine a note of suspicion in his voice?

"I really enjoyed it. Met a bunch of new people. Had fun. Went canoeing and almost drowned. Except some guy saved me. That was kind of freaky."

"Hey, I'd like to meet this guy. Thank him for keeping you safe." Troy squeezed her hand a little tighter.

"He was a really nice guy," Emily said, waiting to see Troy's reaction.

"Should I be jealous?"

Emily's heart flipped over again, but she heard the teasing note in his voice, and with a flood of relief she realized he didn't know. Nicole hadn't phoned him like she had threatened to.

"No. You don't need to be jealous at all. He's just a friend. We talked a bunch because he lost his mother too."

"So you had a lot in common," Troy said quietly, stroking his thumb over her hand.

Emily could have kissed him right then and there. He understood. He got it.

She told him about Mike. Told him about camp and what an experience it was for her. He told her about work. They talked about friends and made plans for the coming week. They talked for more than an hour, their conversation slipping into an easy rhythm.

Then suddenly Troy glanced at his watch. "Sorry, Emily. I gotta take off. I have to go in to work. But I really wanted to see you first."

"I'm glad you came," Emily said.

"Me too." Troy stood up and then bent over the table and dropped a kiss on her forehead. "See you later?"

"For sure."

He tucked a strand of hair behind her ear and then walked away, whistling. Emily watched him go, all the burdens of the past few days melting in the warmth of his smile and understanding.

She got up and glanced back to where Nicole was sitting, thinking again that Nicole hadn't called Troy at all. She'd just been playing Emily along.

Suddenly Emily had had enough. She would finish this once and for all. She strode over to Nicole's seat before she lost her nerve and the anger that sent her there. The diner wasn't very full, and that would make this a lot easier.

Nicole looked up. Then her eyes narrowed when she saw Emily.

"What do you want?" Nicole asked in a haughty tone. "Why are you bothering me?"

Emily stared down at her and then sighed.

This was a waste of time. Nicole didn't like her. Never would. She was about to leave when Nicole looked at her again, and in that look Emily saw the glimmer of an unfamiliar emotion that made her pause. It was as if Nicole wanted something from Emily. The last time Emily'd seen that look, Nicole had wanted to befriend her—for her own selfish reasons. She hadn't trust her since.

"How's Troy? I'm guessing you figured out I didn't call him from camp," Nicole said in a self-righteous tone, fiddling with the scarf wrapped around her neck.

"You're guessing right," Emily said. She took another look at Nicole's scarf and then smiled. It was identical to the one she had bought only a couple of weeks ago at the dollar store. And the earrings looked a lot like the ones Emily had found in the half-price bin at Brenda's Clothing Store in Bedford.

Her mind skipped back to what Ashley had said, and what Mike had told her. Was Nicole really jealous? Was she really trying to imitate Emily?

And in that moment, all the things she had learned at camp came together. All the things about love and caring and seeing Jesus in other people and not putting herself first.

To her surprise, she suddenly felt sorry for Nicole. And even more surprising, the anger that had launched her out of her seat to give Nicole a piece of her mind was now gone. Instead she found herself praying, hoping God would give her patience and understanding.

Emily made a sudden decision. She sat across from Nicole, took a breath, and plunged in.

"Why don't you like me, Nicole?"

Nicole shot her a puzzled glance. As if she didn't know what Emily was talking about.

"Ever since I moved to Bedford, you've been kind of

mean to me." Emily struggled to temper her words. To think of Nicole as a person she should care about.

"Well ... you made that nasty comment about the food my mother served in the cafeteria."

"And I apologized for that."

"And then there was the Christmas play and ... and ..." Nicole stuttered, struggling to find another offense.

Emily had to press her lips together as all the mean things Nicole had done and said to her popped into her mind.

It's not about you, she reminded herself. *This is about Nicole.*

"But none of those things were mean or nasty," Emily said, trying to keep her voice low. Trying not to get angry. "And if I did hurt you, I'd like you to let me know how."

Nicole's eyes narrowed. "You think you're so much better than us, don't you?"

Emily felt as if she had been slapped. "No. I don't. Why do you think that?"

"The way you dress. Like you have to be different."

Nicole looked at Emily's outfit—the shirt she had designed and sewn herself.

"Why is that bad?"

Nicole fidgeted with her own scarf, her lips pursing. "I ... it just is."

"Don't *you* want to be different?" Emily asked.

Nicole glanced at her shirt again, and Emily caught a flash of something else in her eyes. Almost like Nicole wanted it for herself.

Emily bit her lip, a part of her wishing she hadn't heard all those lessons on caring for someone and turning the other cheek and especially the one about how, if someone takes your coat, you should give him your shirt too.

Now something else caught hold of her. Something bigger. Something more important than her own needs and wants. After everything she'd experienced at camp, she didn't want to fall back into the same nasty patterns now that she was home. Something had to change, and if Nicole wouldn't then it was up to her.

Emily leaned forward and tugged her arms out of the sleeves of her shirt—quickly, before she changed her mind. She pulled it off, folded it up, and handed it to Nicole.

"Do you want this?"

Nicole's eyes got big, her mouth fell open.

Emily laid it on the table in front of her, feeling a tinge of regret as she let go. "You can have it if you want. I've only worn it a couple of times. So it's kind of new. Consider it a peace offering." Giving Nicole the shirt wasn't as easy to do as she had hoped, but once she took her hands off it, she actually felt pretty good.

"But . . . I don't think—"

"You don't have to take it."

But Nicole laid her hand on the shirt, her lower lip caught between her teeth. She took a slow breath, like she wasn't sure what to say.

"I can't believe you just gave this to me," she said, her voice hushed. "Are you sure?"

Emily nodded, feeling more sure each moment. "Yes. I'm positive. I want you to have it, and I want you to enjoy it."

Nicole's hand moved over the shirt, as if testing to see if

it was real. Then she turned to Emily and gave her a funny look. Like she'd like to smile at Emily but didn't really know how.

"Thank you, Emily." And for once, that sarcastic note was missing from her voice, which was as good as a smile as far as Emily was concerned.

"You're welcome, Nicole."

If this were a television show or a sappy movie, this would be the part where they would hug and say they would never fight again. That they would be best friends, and then maybe they'd find a field of flowers to run through together.

But this was a diner in Bedford.

And Nicole was still, well, Nicole.

Emily got up and smiled at Nicole. "I hope you enjoy it," she said. Then she walked out of the diner, her heart light.

Chapter Nineteen

"Do you think it will rain?" Christopher asked, looking up at the sky. A few dark clouds drifted across the sun, making him shiver.

"It will be fine. The forecast for the Fourth of July is for hot, sunny weather," Grandpa said with a grin. "Those clouds are moving away. Now let's go find our float and get it ready to go."

Uncle Pete and Sam had left early this morning to drive the float to the parade grounds on time. Everyone else had come later in the truck.

As they passed by the gathered floats, Christopher checked them out.

One held only a great big "4", for July 4, decorated in red, white, and blue sparkles, and behind it, a bunch of American flags were folded to look like a huge fan.

Another one was just a fence with some goats. A boy with leather pants and a funny little hat was trying to keep them under control.

The float he liked best was built like a big, white swan covered with paper flowers. A couple of pretty girls in long dresses stood by it, fussing with each other's hair.

His own stomach growled. Grandma had tried to make him eat breakfast, but he couldn't. He was too nervous.

As Christopher followed Grandpa to the wagon a steady buzz of chatter and laughter surrounded them. His nervous flutters got bigger.

"Where's our float?" Christopher looked around. "Are you sure Sam and Uncle Pete got here?"

Grandpa squeezed his shoulder. "I know they did. Because there it is." Grandpa pointed, and then, just behind a wagon with a bunch of little kids on it, he saw the tractor, and behind it the Heather Creek Farm float.

He tried not to feel too proud as they got closer.

Aunt Dana had painted the little wooden shed white to make it look like a house. Uncle Pete had put in a little window, and Grandma had put a box of fake flowers below it.

Emily had made some curtains for the window and a tablecloth for the little table that held a couple of loaves of bread. She'd also sewed up some aprons and skirts for her and Grandma to wear.

Grandpa had oiled the rust off the plow and painted the handles a bright red. Aunt Dana had found a bunch of wheat stems around the farm.

They were tied up and standing in a row between the seeder and the scythe Sam would be using instead of the flail. When the whole family started helping, they all agreed the flail was too dangerous to swing around. Grandpa had found an old scythe that he and Uncle Pete fixed up for Sam to hold instead.

Uncle Pete had decided he would pretend to seed with the hand seeder. Grandma and Emily would stand by the house with the bread.

Everyone else was already at the float when he and Grandpa got there. Aunt Dana, Uncle Pete, and Sam walked around the float, making sure everything was attached and arranged properly.

"Here they are," Emily said when she spotted Christopher and Grandpa. She waved her bonnet at them and then hiked up her long skirt and climbed down off the hay wagon. "Grandma wants to know if you want her to pretend to slice the bread, or just hold it?"

"Just hold it. Then she can wave at the people."

"This is yours." Emily plopped an old battered straw hat onto his head and grinned; then she glanced back at the float. "This is pretty exciting, little brother," she said. "I can't believe you thought of this all by yourself."

"I had some help from Aunt Dana."

Emily gave him a quick hug. "Maybe, but you did a lot of the work too. I'm so proud of you."

Christopher's heart got all big in his chest, and his smile grew wide. "Thanks, Emily."

"How do I look?" She twirled in front of him, her long dress flowing around her legs. It was made of bright blue material scattered with pink flowers. He hadn't thought his sister would ever wear something like that, but she had picked the material out herself from Aunt Rosemary's shop.

"Like a pioneer lady."

"Just the look I was going for." She winked at Christopher. "Are you ready to get this show on the road?"

"I'm ready." He took a deep breath and rubbed his hands over his pants. He sort of felt ready, but his stomach was fluttering kind of funny. He hoped he wouldn't faint again.

Emily grabbed his hand and squeezed it. "Don't look so worried, Christopher. This is going to be great. You did a fantastic job." Then she gave him a big hug and a kiss, making his hat go all crooked on his head. "And look, we're float number five. How cool is that?" She pointed at the number that was attached to the front bucket of the tractor.

That was even more exciting to know. People wouldn't be bored with the parade by the time they came by.

The parade marshal came by and told them all to get ready. Christopher walked over to Aunt Dana, who was rearranging the bunches of wheat.

"We have to go," he said to her.

She nodded but kept fiddling.

"You *are* coming on the float with us, aren't you?" he asked. Yesterday Aunt Dana had said there might not be enough room for her.

Aunt Dana patted him on the shoulder. "I think it's more important that you all do this as a family."

"But you're part of our family," Christopher said.

"I know, but you have enough people," Aunt Dana said. "And I know you wanted it to look just right."

Christopher looked back over his shoulder. Yes, there *were* a lot of people on the wagon, but he didn't care. He turned back to her. "It will only look just right if you're on it. Besides, you're the only one who helped me from the beginning."

Aunt Dana smiled and was looking like she was going to say no again when Emily and Grandma joined them. "C'mon, Dana," Grandma said. "It's time to go."

"I thought maybe just the family should be on the float," Aunt Dana said.

Grandma made a noise that sounded like a snort. "And you're part of our family too, Mrs. Stevenson."

"You're being silly," Emily said, catching her by the arm. "We've got to get going."

Aunt Dana looked from Emily to Grandma to Christopher, grinned, and climbed up on the float.

When they were all ready, Grandpa gave them a signal, put the tractor in gear, and with a jerk, they were going. Christopher grabbed the plow and then looked behind him. Uncle Pete was already cranking the handle of the seeder, and Sam was making little swinging motions with the scythe.

And now everyone, his whole family was all here with him: Sam, Emily, Grandma and Grandpa, Uncle Pete and Aunt Dana. Just like he had pictured it in his mind and didn't think would happen. This was so exciting.

The float moved along and then turned down the street. Butterflies danced in Christopher's stomach when he saw the rows of people lining the sidewalks.

All looking at them.

He heard a cheer and someone call his name. He saw Dylan Lonetree with his family waving at him. Christopher waved back.

More cheers.

Then he heard someone yell, "Hey, Slater. Lookin' pretty cool."

Christopher looked over to where the voice came from and saw a tall teenager standing with his hands in the back pockets of his blue jeans. He was smiling, but it wasn't a friendly smile. More like a poking-fun smile. A mean, poking-fun smile. A guy beside him pretended to be doing what Sam did, but he had the same mean smile on his face.

Christopher looked frantically over at Sam, hoping he wouldn't get mad. Hoping Sam wouldn't quit.

But Sam wasn't even looking at the guys. He just kept pretending to scythe. He took his hat off and pretended to wipe his forehead, rolled his shoulders, and started again. Then he caught Christopher's eye and winked.

It's okay, Christopher thought. *It's all okay.*

He looked ahead, holding the plow, feeling a burst of pride and happiness. They were really here. They were really in the parade, on a float that he and Aunt Dana had dreamed up.

They were celebrating their country's birthday as a family. Just like he had hoped would happen.

He waved at the people, his heart bursting in his chest. Today was a great day. A wonderful day. A happy birthday to America day.

"ARE YOU SURE this is the best place to watch the fireworks?" Charlotte clutched the blanket, looking over her shoulder. "I'm wondering if Frank and Hannah can find us here. I wonder if I should go down . . ."

"Grandpa is waiting for them," Emily interrupted, taking the blanket from her hands. "He can take care of that."

Charlotte nodded, recognizing that Emily was right. How long would it take her to learn that she didn't need to do it all?

Maybe my whole life.

"Do you think he'll be able to find us?" she couldn't help but add.

"How could he miss us?" Emily said, pointing to the glow-in-the-dark band that she and everyone else wore on their heads.

"No, I guess we're pretty obvious," Charlotte said.

"If you're just going to yak, give me the blanket and I'll lay it out." Troy took the blanket from Emily, but Charlotte saw the teasing glimmer in his eyes as he did.

He was a good kid. Emily had told her about their conversation in the diner and how understanding he had been. Sure, Emily was a bit young, but who knew? She and Bob had been high school sweethearts.

"Just relax and sit down," Emily said as she pressed gently on Charlotte's shoulders. "Aunt Dana made us a thermos of lemonade and I brought cups and napkins. Troy and I are going to get them from the truck, and *you* are supposed to stay here."

"Okay. I will." She did as she was commanded, feeling a little funny that all she had to do was show up.

As Troy and Emily walked away in the gathering dusk, she glanced down the hill, wondering where Bob was. Had something happened to Frank and Hannah? Maybe she should go check. She got up just as Sam came puffing up the hill.

"Grandma, what are you doing?" Sam came through the crowd to stand in front of Charlotte.

"Um ... nothing."

Sam wasn't buying it. "Just checking to see if Grandpa is coming and thinking maybe you should go down and see what's happening?" he asked with a teasing note in his voice.

Charlotte shot him a frown but then had to smile at the mischief in his eyes highlighted by the green glow of his headband. "Okay. As you would say, busted."

"You don't have to do it all, you know." Sam gave her a light punch on her shoulder, and then gently pushed her back down onto the blanket. He sat beside her, looping his arms around his knees, and suddenly seemed to grow serious. He looked away, rocking lightly.

"You know, Grandma, I said I was sorry about what happened. But I feel like I need to say it again," he said quietly.

Charlotte resisted the urge to lay her hand on his arm. To try to ease his discomfort. She sensed he needed to speak his mind. Again.

"I made a mistake. And I'd like to think I won't make any more mistakes, but I'd also like to think I'm trying not to," he said, his deep voice lowering even more. "I know I have a lot of growing up to do." He sighed lightly and then looked over at Charlotte. "But I have some good examples."

Charlotte held his gaze, feeling the prick of happy tears in her eyes. "I don't know about that," she returned. "I'm always learning myself. Always recognizing that every day I have to let go of things and let God take over."

Sam nodded slowly, as if absorbing what she was saying.

"I'm proud of you," Charlotte continued. "I heard your friends teasing you when you were on the float."

Sam shrugged, as if unwilling to take her compliment. "They weren't friends of mine. Just some guys who were at the party."

The sound of laughter floated up the hill from the people gathering for the fireworks. A gentle peace slipped over Charlotte as the darkness deepened. "I also got a call from Mr. Vance, the owner of the cottage. He wanted me to know that he was grateful for your help. He also said that it was very brave of you to show up."

"I went because you told me to, Grandma. And Grandpa even drove me out there. I shouldn't get any credit for that." Sam shot her a quick sideways glance. "But I'm glad you made me go. It was a way to make up for my stupidity and poor judgment."

Charlotte slipped her arm around Sam's shoulders and gave him a quick hug. "You're not stupid, my dear boy. I want to share with you one of my favorite sayings: 'Good judgment comes from experience. And experience comes from poor judgment.' So if you think of it that way, you're on your way to making good judgments."

Sam laughed at that. "I'll keep that in mind." He straightened, looking down the hill. "And you don't need to worry anymore about Grandpa and Mr. and Mrs. Carter finding us."

"There you are," Charlotte heard Hannah saying.

Charlotte saw three figures slowly making their way up the hill. Frank was walking with a walker, and Hannah carried a backpack and a blanket. She waved as they came closer. "I brought cookies," she said.

"Great," Sam said with a short laugh. "Just what I need on top of two funnel cakes and two hot dogs."

"You had two funnel cakes?" Emily said incredulously as she and Troy materialized seemingly out of nowhere, carrying a cooler between them.

"My stomach hurts just thinking about that," Uncle Pete said as he, Dana, and Christopher arrived.

"But *you* had four corn dogs, Uncle Pete," Christopher said. "That would make me even sicker than two funnel cakes."

"I'll tell you what would make me the sickest of all, Christopher, my boy," Uncle Pete said as he dropped onto the blanket beside Sam. "Going on that ride that you and Sam thought was just the bomb."

"It was," Christopher exclaimed. "Right, Sam?"

"Oh, yeah. Especially after two funnel cakes," Sam said with a wry note in his voice.

General laughter followed that comment as everyone settled down in their respective spots. Then Charlotte caught Sam frowning at Christopher's pants. "Are those the ones you wore on the float?"

Christopher hastily covered the knee of one leg and shot Charlotte a guilty glance. "I'm sorry, Grandma."

"You ripped them again?" Emily said. "After Grandma spent so much time patching them?" She sighed and glanced at Charlotte. "I don't know how you do it, Grandma."

Sometimes, neither did Charlotte.

"Frank, how are you doing?" Charlotte asked as Hannah laid out her blanket.

"I'm doing great," he said. "Doc said I can start physical therapy soon. Heart's lookin' pretty good. If I was feeling any better, I'd be twins."

Charlotte grinned, catching Hannah's wink. "He's just glad to be out of the house," Hannah said.

"And we're glad you could join us for the fireworks,"

Bob said, lowering himself slowly beside Charlotte. "We should have brought some chairs," he added, grunting as he sat down.

"We've always watched fireworks sitting on a blanket," Pete said. "That way we can lie down if our necks get sore."

"We're sitting high enough," Dana put in. "We shouldn't have to look up."

"Last year some of them went way up into the sky," Christopher said, waving his arm to underline his comment. "And then we got sore necks."

Charlotte leaned back on her elbows, glancing around the gathered group, smiling as the conversation grew louder, split off into two or three, doubled back, and joined up again.

Dana and Emily served up the lemonade and Hannah's cookie tin was passed back and forth, each time losing a few more cookies.

Then the first whiz sounded, followed by various pops and booms; suddenly brightly colored bursts of light showered upward and outward into the darkness.

"Whoa, that was a big one."

More showers of pink and purple filled the sky, following whizzes and bangs as mortars screamed upward, incandescent green blazing in their wake.

Each new burst brought an exclamation of amazement and admiration from the crowd.

Charlotte's attention turned from the display above her to the faces around her, sporadically illuminated by the light.

Emily, Troy, and Sam were grinning; Christopher had his

hands clasped under his chin. Pete and Dana stole a kiss when they thought no one was looking. Bob was smiling, and Frank and Hannah both looked happy.

It had happened, Charlotte thought, taking another sip of her cold lemonade. Her family had come together in love and happiness for this holiday celebration. And she had done very little to bring it about. It had come together organically because they were a family. A family that wanted to be together and do things together because they loved each other.

She looked up as an especially loud burst of fireworks split the night.

Thank You, Lord, she prayed silently, watching the display. *Thank You for my family, for my country, for my life.*

About the Author

Carolyne Aarsen is the author of over sixty books and counting and not ready to quit any time soon. Some of her books include not only the Home to Heather Creek series but also the Tales from Grace Chapel Inn series put out by Guideposts, as well as numerous books for Love Inspired. She lives on a farm close to the hamlet of Neerlandia where she and her husband have raised four children and taken in numerous foster children. She is currently self-published and enjoying that journey far more than she expected.

A Note from the Editors

We hope you enjoyed this volume in the Home to Heather Creek series, published by Guideposts. For over seventy-five years, Guideposts, a nonprofit organization, has been driven by a vision of a world filled with hope. We aspire to be the voice of a trusted friend, a friend who makes you feel more hopeful and connected.

By making a purchase from Guideposts, you join our community in touching millions of lives, inspiring them to believe that all things are possible through faith, hope, and prayer. Your continued support allows us to provide uplifting resources to those in need.

Whether through our online communities, websites, apps, or publications, we strive to inspire our audiences, bring them together, and comfort, uplift, entertain, and guide them.

To learn more, please go to guideposts.org.

Find inspiration, find faith, find Guideposts.

Shop our best sellers and favorites at
guideposts.org/shop

Or scan the QR code to go directly to our Shop